NEXT GENERATION

NEXT GENERATION

Travels in Israel

David Pryce-Jones

HOLT, RINEHART AND WINSTON

New York   Chicago   San Francisco

Copyright © 1964 by David Pryce-Jones

First published in the United States in 1965
Library of Congress Catalog Card Number: 65-14444

Chapter 1 was originally published as "Israel's Three Cities" in
Commentary, and a much-abbreviated article on "The Yossele Case"
appeared in the *New Statesman.* Passages from Chapter 10 were included in an article for the *Spectator.* The author is grateful for
permission to reprint.

First Edition

87202-0215

Printed in the United States of America

CONTENTS

For C. and J. who came too.

PREFACE

IN THE GROWING LITERATURE about Israel, there is more than sufficient record of its political history, of the economic factors governing the country's development, of its debt to the ancient heredity of its religion, down to analyses of the Histadrut operations, the organizations of the kibbutz movement and the voting figures in the last Knesset. Whatever else an observer may feel about Israel, if his curiosity is aroused, there is already a massive amount of printed work, from the specific thesis to the general survey, to satisfy him. The circumstances surrounding Zionist aspirations and the creation and continued growth of the state of Israel have been so integral a part of recent history that opinion on these subjects has been proportionately diffuse, and it therefore seems unnecessary to go over familiar ground, particularly at a moment when Israel is emerging from past vicissitudes and consolidating as an independent, increasingly self-reliant country.

1948 saw the violent end of the British Mandate. But the violence was also due to the internal pressure which brought the Jewish minority into a position of domination over the Arab majority. This then, was not the now familiar issue of a colonial power handing over to a hitherto subject people and, in so many words, telling them to get on with it. This involved a question of survival for the Jews, irrespective

7

of rights and wrongs, an opposition of moralities, a tragedy of history which found no issue except in a trial of strength. Fifteen years have passed, during which these events have taken on a longer perspective. For complex political reasons, the Arab refugee problem—the wretched legacy from the war—is no nearer solution. But meanwhile the state of Israel has taken shape, and put down roots in the Middle East which have a hold in the soil. Whatever its detractors say, or hope, Israel is here to stay, unless there is a holocaust of such disaster that it becomes irrelevant which countries have been eliminated. A new personality is evolving as a new generation grows up, which has less intimate memories of past tragedies but a more acute perception of Middle East realities.

My purpose was to discover what might be the characteristics of this Second Generation, to try to understand what are the human tensions, the desires and aspirations and anxieties, which are stitching a ramified past into a common present. This is an exceptional country whose character changes fast, as its exceptional circumstances dictate. The unique fusion of people and place is turning the Jew into the Israeli, however intricate and emotional and indispensable the remaining links with the Diaspora may be. A social artificiality has hardened into a way of life, aided—indeed inspired—by Arab hostility which has paradoxically not been without benefit to Israel, quickening the Israeli self-awareness and defensiveness, forging the new identity under a sense of danger, enabling it to find a coherent expression. To this extent the Arabs have helped to create those characteristics of the Israelis which they most fear and dislike, just as Europeans before them created what they believed to have been characteristic of the Jews. But apart from the campaign of 1956, there has been a recent lull in the almost continuous fighting or rioting since the Balfour Declaration of 1917 and a generation has grown up in comparative peace, establishing itself at any rate by Israeli standards, in something like security. But the immigration of Oriental Jews, the dispossessed inhabitants of Arab countries, has been intensive during the last ten years and by 1970 these are expected to account for some three-quarters of the population. This will involve yet another technical, economic and cultural readjustment which might prove a threat to the internal stability and progress of the country. But this is not a book about the Third Generation and incipient Levantinism, and whenever these are a reality, this book will have been dated by the change. At the moment everybody in Israel has a story to tell, although it is a measure of their involvement both with the past and the future that often they are unwilling to tell it. There are no statistics for happiness or misery, for longings or for the strength of the will to survive. Hence I make no apologies for refining the experiences of my travels into the form of single cohesive chapters which derive either from my own observation, or from my attention in listening to other people's stories when I could. This seemed to be the best way to catch the transience of the moment, of the mood, to feel the undercurrent of Israeli life as it presented itself to someone living over a period in the country. This naturally implies selectivity and accordingly I have left out what I believed did not help to recreate the Israeli atmosphere. In its way, this is a travel book although only three chapters, In the Cities, Yossele Schumacher and The Last Word are strictly reportage. The remaining chapters conceal the identities of close friends and acquaintances and chance meetings, and I have therefore taken some liberties with personalities, in the belief that what they stood for or what they represented in particular, was also a predicament or context common to many others in Israel. The curious, depending on their inclinations or prejudices, will find what I have left out in the Government Year Books, the official publications and the authorized histories—Zionist, Arab, British or United Nations—in the propaganda which we like to use as a dressing to cover up the way in which we behave one towards another.

Chapter One

IN THE CITIES

THE MEETING POINT OF Haifa is the observation platform in the middle of Panorama Road. It is always crowded. People come casually to stare at the most spectacular sweep of the Mediterranean in Israel, and go away surfeited. It is a purpose in itself. Almost every day, a very old man, accompanied by two students from a neighbouring *yeshiva*, comes there to read on one of the benches. And every morning and evening an Arab woman rides past on her donkey, keeping her back to the view both on the way up and down.

A view needs to be related in order to be understood, otherwise it will disintegrate to pinpricks dancing before the eyes. In Haifa the reference points are the oil refineries, the docks, the immense Dagon storehouse, the stacks of the cement works, and beyond everything, the bland vista of the sea. The eye, accustomed to staring out, naturally moves beyond these industrial fixities and takes in the ships. Not the liners ceremoniously coming and going with African heads of states, but the immigrant ships working regular passages. The observation platform cannot break through its limitations: at that height the number of funnels is all that matters. But immigration is the unconscious rhythm of Haifa.

The mechanism is now so smooth that it passes almost unnoticed in the town. It requires some ingenuity to discover the dates of arrival. A ship docks at six in the morning and is cleared by ten. Everything is now geared to make these routines as inconspicuous as possible. Bureaucratic efficiency is counteracted only by groups of charitable ladies and high-school children sent as welcoming parties, detailed to carry the hand luggage. For them it is a morning's outing. The trucks drive the immigrants away, the ship is prepared for sea; the pulse goes on.

Haifa has abruptly changed its character in the last fourteen years: a different city has been superimposed on the old Arab town, like a second, stronger exposure on the negative of a photograph. At both stages, though, as far as the state of Israel is concerned, the natural function of the place has been to absorb immigrants. Haifa itself deliberately ignores this process. It is through this tacit indifference to the changing population that Israeli conservatism has evolved. Conservatism in Israel is a shield against the present and the future, and it seems to operate particularly in Haifa. It is a defence against the influences of protracted and successive waves of immigrants, all of which inevitably impede organic growth of the new community. In the absence of more embracing reference points, the small ethnic communities in turn remain heterogeneous, clinging to whatever can be maintained from previous ways of life. This conservatism is self-protective, a social withdrawal.

Some law of social accretion, of bottleneck, has hemmed in the Sephardic immigrants from North Africa, as if they had been unable to disperse farther than the quarters surrounding the docks where they landed. They have moved into the old abandoned Arab town, spreading behind the port and northward to the industrial zone. Much of this housing was badly damaged, and the whole district is still cased with rubble from half-cleared *souks*, with sections of houses trimmed away, or supported by a few arches which have not yet collapsed, and steps leading unevenly up to nothing. All this breeds among the inhabitants a sense of identity, more particularly as the new housing begins immediately to rise like an affront behind this anachronism of a *casbah*, while Technion City stands smug on the hills behind.

The sense of identity is indeed formidable, compounded out of difficult conflicts which continue to fester in the enclosed streets. The principle tension is between nostalgia and resentment. For Moroccans, Tunisians and Algerians, this often goes with the claim of being French: the mood of frustration is much like that of the *pieds-noirs* crowding into Marseilles, spreading along the coast of the Midi. Conversations begin with stories of Arab injustices and petty tyrannies, the drainage of constant bribery and protection money to patriot-thugs. 'I got some money out by jamming it into the soles of my shoes. What they could see, they took.' Or a long story of selling and reselling a business, a café, in order to register owners under different names, sharing the money into complicated percentages in order to rescue something. Yet the talk ends on a note of evocation, the memories of a continuity now shattered. The patent resentment of these Sephardic Jews is against the Arabs who compelled them to sign off a long and involved past, breaking familiar patterns: the richer immigrants went to France, the majority to Israel. From the other side, it is inevitably with these poorer strata of society that most Israeli Arabs come into daily contact. This is the cradle of aggressive nationalism, a desire to get revenge based on fear and a broken way of life.

In the meantime there is the new life not of their making, and in the face of the readjustments which it demands, there is every excuse for withdrawal. Hence the touchiness, the quick grievances, the occasional violence provoked by anything which appears to interfere. This volatility is another tension keeping the Sephardic community in uneasy ferment. It breaks out spasmodically, in such instances as a riot not long ago when a drunken Moroccan was involved in a brawl with a policeman. The word ran round the quarter that an Ashkenazi was ill-treating a Sephardi and spontaneously a crowd gathered to march on Haifa, breaking windows and destroying property. Such outbursts are rare, but a kind of promiscuous violence is latent in the area. Evidence for it may be read on posters displaying rabble-rousing sentiments: 'A year has passed, a year of preparation, a year of training for carrying out the sublime mission we have undertaken—Complete Equality for all the Jews in Israel! Smashing the conspiracy to set up two classes of citizens in Israel. . . . We do not want Sephardim-Ashkenazim. We do want one constructive people.'

In other towns where there are similar extensive Sephardic communities, Beersheba for instance, this particular provocative unease has not blanketed daily existence in quite the same way, despite the same large families and the same overcrowding. These communities outside Haifa seem more ready to meet circumstances with an acceptance which, even if passive, holds hope for the future. The old Haifa slums, wedging their inhabitants into the rubbish-laden confines between the Wadi Salib and the Wadi Nisnis, convince them that the former Arab discrimination might not have proved so difficult to combat as the new indifference, the cold-shouldering, to which there is no comeback.

Growing up in this milieu, the Haifa youth possess that mixture of aggression and boredom which is the hallmark of their European counterpart. Some of the characteristics are acquired from the port, although there is nothing comparable to the belt of underworld parasites of Naples and Marseilles. Haifa's young men are, by comparison, well-mannered and socially responsible, clinging together and rarely trying to intimidate anyone but themselves. Most of the youths who gather in the streets are seeking no more than a personality of their own, or even a little privacy, away from their huge families. The small groups of real teddy boys among them take to mild delinquency; a favourite if not especially lucrative racket is to obtain blocks of cinema seats and resell them at black-market prices on crowded evenings outside the box-office which is resolutely turning the customers away. Clothes, mannerisms, haircuts, are a few years out of date, imitations of old European fashions. Black leather jackets are now *in* among the Armon Commandos, named after the cinema where they cluster, rowdies not hooligans, and untypical of Israeli life.

Once I saw a punch-up in a crowded Tel Aviv street between two very brawny young men, capable of hurting each other badly. A diminutive army colonel stepped out of the night and separated them, sending them reluctantly on their way, and even flashing old-fashioned rebukes at them from behind his pebble-glass spectacles. The Armon Commandos seem to have passed beyond the arbitration of stray colonels. In Haifa too, there is more of an acceptance of violence. At a wedding in a large café near the port, the garden was boarded round to keep away staring onlookers. The crowd collected at the back, jostling to look through the kitchen window. While a fat but youngish woman was pressing into the best position, a heavy knob attached to the curtain rail inside swung loose and smashed a pane of glass. A kitchen-boy of about ten threw the knob at her, breaking more glass. When she shouted at him, he spat in her eye and picked up a long sliver of glass like a scimitar to attack her. She leant through the broken window to cuff him, while the crowd watched the fight impassively. Several old men in pyjamas were standing on the corner, connoisseurs of such scenes.

Bourgeois children react differently to the lack of social integration. As Haifa hardens into set class or income patterns, it becomes more and more common to discover a well-off family reluctantly accepting a son's decision not to follow an established line. There are not so many *fils à papa* prepared to absorb the Haifa conservatism. Reaction becomes rebellion only when there is an ethos against which the inexperienced cannot prevail. Haifa accentuates the ambiguous attitude towards urban life almost endemic in young Israelis, that the city offers material advantages, prospects, domesticity, culture and pleasure—in equal proportions to corruption. To their children, the elder generation appear to have imposed hierarchical and fossilized clamps on the life of the city to produce a system which outwardly resembles those they formerly understood. Only occasional chinks show in the well-protected outward appearance, as for instance in the recent Chicago-style episode in the Haifa slaughterhouse when one worker shot dead a rival who was trying to break the municipal monopoly and then committed suicide. 'Who'd stay in a town like that?' one young *kibbutznik* whose family lived in Haifa said to me shortly after the murder.

Some of the more unremitting clamps derive from the self-imposed conservatism. Not long ago I went to a kibbutz wedding where the bridegroom was the son of Haifa industrialists who had done their best to prevent him from becoming a member of this kibbutz. In the face of the inevitable, however, the Haifa family and their friends arrived at the kibbutz for the wedding, only to fall immediately on the food and practically devour it all, even before the ceremony was over. By the time a second, subsequent wedding service had been performed, there was no food left. This behaviour would have been more understandable, complained the kibbutz members, if the guests had not been so fat and obviously well fed. The last straw was the surprise shown by these guests that the kibbutz was able to provide such good food. Hadn't they called in an outside caterer?

Haifa's insulation from the rest of the country has become more marked, paradoxically, with the general improvement of communications. The port city was once the centre for the kibbutzim and settlements of the hinterland, of the Emek. Now that Tel Aviv is so much more accessible, Haifa has less to offer and consequently receives less. The visitors mill about on the observation platform and then go home. There is nothing else to do.

It is not only the behaviour of Haifa businessmen and their families at a kibbutz wedding which heightens the impression that the city has stratified and hardened class lines. Haifa is dominated by its middle-class ethos, most evident in the materialism generated in this prosperous industrial city. The dissatisfaction of the young is the result of living amidst the embodiment of those aspects of the future which call for something other than the virtues inculcated by contemporary Israeli ideals. And there is no going back. The weakening of its ties with the surrounding countryside brings to the fore the accusation of provincialism which is usually levelled against Haifa. What is intended by this, it seems, is a protest against the emergence of a European industrial city.

There can be few examples of social status corresponding so nicely to geographical elevation. The road up the Carmel rises like a Mediterranean *corniche* through a landscape of rock and pine, from *shikunim* to villas, from dense living to pretty gardens and watered lawns that overlook the roofs below. In between the clutter at the bottom of the mountain and the view at the top stand the former houses of rich Arabs, now mostly public buildings and institutions. There are also the isolated Mandate buildings, apeing their English Home Counties originals, with a few foreign-inspired exceptions like the *art-nouveau* villa of the Templars. And at the hub, like a tropical spider cocooned in its web, is the Bahai Temple, that small gold-domed Taj Mahal, with a baby Acropolis sheltering next to it. This exotic fantasy is wonderfully out of place, expensive and empty, with a brown-pyjamaed janitor to shepherd visitors past the photographs of Persian and Turkish dignitaries, stylized in frock-coat and *tarbush*. In the close-built streets around the Hadar Carmel dwell the professionals and skilled workers, in all their gradations of status. The houses are linked by steep flights of stone steps up the mountain, inducing a sense of neighbourhood, of links, which is sometimes reminiscent of Naples. But here the life is quiet, domestic, early to bed and early to rise, with the due rewards. The streets are virtually deserted after nightfall; small groups sit on balconies, drink coffee and talk in discreet undertones.

Higher up the mountain it is not so very different. The balconies are more secluded: the circles of friends are not much wider nor is the conversation much more animated. Here is the fullest bourgeois existence, cherishing no standards and no aims beyond those of correctness and personal satisfaction, and happy within these controls. If parts of the Carmel are a subdued and orderly Naples, the top is a Mediterranean Zürich or Geneva. Some of the villas, particularly along the summit towards Ahuza, are large and luxurious, all chromium and glass and air-conditioning. Their owners are the Haifa tycoons, living well, but without the conspicuous consumption of the rich elsewhere. They content themselves with the comparatively unostentatious comfort of the two cars, a maid and a gardener (who are often Druzes), the small collection of Hellenistic antiquities in the living-room and the broken statuary in the garden.

With exceptions, the social life is marked by a slightly awkward formality, the result of lingering European inhibitions. Houses are visited in rotation, hospitality reciprocated accordingly. It is perhaps another aspect of the self-defence mechanism. Such thoughtless behaviour as that of the wedding party at the kibbutz, for instance, derives from a nervous insecurity about how one ought to behave on such occasions in such unusual company. There is a real ignorance which cannot be met by any former experience, and it is too late in the day to learn. A significant proportion of this middle-class element does not speak Hebrew. The women especially make little or no effort to learn even after many years, unless for the purpose of going shopping. And perhaps it is unnecessary for them, because as nearly as possible a way of existence has been reconstructed which makes the minimum concessions to the new Israeli society. Just as there is an Arabic-speaking Sephardic community, so there is a cohesive Russian community, far removed from the values of a pioneering Aliyah. Their conversation is of Pasternak and of the portraits painted by the poet's father. Or of Nabokov and his early untranslated novels and the incomprehensibility of *Lolita*. And there is the German-speaking community—distinct from the Yiddish-speaking—

quoting Goethe and wondering about the Bayreuth Festival.

Similar communities may also exist elsewhere, but in a city like Haifa which has so rapidly switched its population and therefore its character, maintaining only an unbroken rhythm of immigration, they exercise a disproportionate influence. In a swirl of mixed and mixing values, the group will predominate which has a fairly firm self-assurance about the kind of life it wants to lead. Tragic disasters have invalidated the past but not eradicated its influences: and in the absence of indigenous tradition, of a specific quality—whatever form it might take—that could be defined as Israeli, an unmistakable part of Haifa looks backward for its points of reference. Hence the tenacious Sephardis and the close-knit Russians, Poles and Germans, and their inability, even unwillingness, to meet. Perhaps it should be called no more than a reserve on all sides, but the defensive at the bottom of the mountain is countered by the tone of patronage at the top. 'It'll be all right in the next generation, after they've sent their children to school.' This is the excuse usually offered for abstaining from the problem: as in all divided societies, the promise of education is the easy panacea, but since high school fees have to be paid by parents, higher knowledge is still the prerogative of the *bourgeoisie*. There is the further distinction that Israelis brought up in Western traditions have a strong and eminent background of scientific and scholastic learning, whereas to the Eastern Jews, to the poorer classes, education is no desideratum, rather the contrary, for it will break up the family unit. And in the interval between the generations come the Armon Commandos, the intransigence towards the Arabs, the parents trying to dissuade their children from joining a kibbutz, the keeping to oneself, the prim conservatism.

The attempt to rebuild life on a once serviceable model produces a weighted sense of social nostalgia which permeates Haifa. And it is virtually the only place in Israel where such a mood prevails, deriving from this reluctance to come to terms with something new. It would be silly to exaggerate so intangible and complicated a set of emotions. The immigration continues: the *shikunim* are filling with hard-headed, progressive and vital workers attracted by the industrial jobs. They do not want such extraneous considerations to interfere with their excellent prospects. For them the garden cities spread around the Carmel, and it is as a result of their self-sufficient attitude that Haifa is also unique in having public transport on the Sabbath. Since the Mandate, labour has dominated the municipal council. In the long run, this may prove the more important factor and turn Haifa's misnomer, 'The City of Workers,' into a reality.

For the present the ladies in polka-dot dresses and elbow-length gloves sitting in the cafés do not share in this spirit; nor do the elderly men with white straw hats and malacca canes exercising their dogs in the evenings; nor the old-timers complaining that things aren't what they were. This is why Haifa seems so cut off, so disparate and dull to the casual observer, so stranded in the landscape, so disturbing; and why people coming to it are vaguely, somewhat inarticulately, critical. Impervious to all such criticism, thousands of inhabitants go about their lives trying not to analyse why they are settled on this particular Mediterranean shore with which they still feel no organic connection, and where there are no roots which they can yet claim for their own. This is what turns Haifa seemingly into an exteriorization, making it appear to be a mere convenience, an observation platform, a place with a superb view across the bay.

II

Tel Aviv is a specifically Israeli growth. Unlike Haifa grafted on top of an Arab town, Tel Aviv has evolved alongside Jaffa—the chimney-stack of the Reading Power Station culminating the northern sweep of the horizon and balancing the Arab minaret on the southern point. It might be expected to evince the characteristics of integration lacking in Haifa and once it probably did, when it was smaller, more manageable, its inhabitants more unified. There has been a population explosion since then which has diversified the city and whose 'accumulation effect' is now manifest. Not only through the direct results of cinemas, newspapers, the four theatres, the business world and big city life in general, but through the heterogeneous social levels. If the pristine image of Tel Aviv is the fading brown and yellow snapshot of early pioneers drawing lots for their sand-plots, a small compact group united in intention, the contemporary image is of an unsettled mass seeking to adapt a fairly uncompromising structure handed down from the past to the varied social needs of the present. Events have moved too quickly for blueprints, modifications, evolutions. Pylons, for instance, which once ran across desert ground, now rise like gigantic street-lamps in central streets which assumed their importance before there was a chance of realigning the grid system. Unfortunately nothing like modern Tel Aviv was ever envisaged and the discrepancies have probably prevented the city fusing into an organic whole: the theories and the assumptions of the Zionist group in the old snapshot with their blend of special nineteenth-century fervour and asceticism, exclusiveness and moral earnestness, are too strong to be dismissed by the external aspects of material progress. The blend has been transmuted certainly but it is still pervasive, so that even when the old values have been forcibly rejected, they are noticeable by their absence.

The old structure is most obvious in the architecture and town-planning of Tel Aviv. Edmund Wilson found that it resembled Athens, but this may be no more than the post-Ottoman heritage, if the old Athens of the Plaka can be equated to Jaffa and its new suburbs to Tel Aviv, unified in both cases by the Mediterranean littoral. The first plans of Tel Aviv took virtually no account of the sea, although it is the major natural feature of the place. Even when these plans were not properly implemented, the sea became important only by default. Swimming is the chief relaxation of the *sabra* generation, and the municipal swimming pool on the edge of the sea is to Tel Aviv what the observation platform is to Haifa. But this, plainly, was inconceivable to the elder generation who planned the city so that the main streets, Hayarkon, Ben Yehuda, Dizengoff, run parallel to the sea, effectively blotting it out. The Samuel Esplanade along the sea-front is a recent gathering together of loose ends. The principle east-west streets are not built to obtain a vista—some, Arlosoroff and Allenby for example, swing away as they near the coast as if positively to obstruct the view. People living and working in Tel Aviv have to remind themselves of its natural situation on the shore. Yet the sea and its breeze are the elements which make the climate of Tel Aviv most supportable. Air is the essential commodity in Tel Aviv, yet the narrow, crowded and airless little streets criss-cross the centre of the town, only occasionally breaking into the open oblong of a *stadtpark*, complete with shrubs and benches and neatly planted trees, as in any Central European town. The houses of three-storey blocks, square and chunky, with balconies stuck out indiscriminately like drawers which will not push shut, cling together in heavy concrete surfaces, baking in the heat. It seems to be the refutation in three dimensions of the formalist argument in architecture. Some modern building breaks the pattern, but the new luxury hotels which form a high chain along the coast epitomize the old manner of turning one's back to the sea. By grabbing the best sites on the coast, these hotels have become an entity halfway between a dyke and a barricade. The suburbs sweeping northwards to the Yarkon river are architecturally more enterprising, although still designed on too small a scale and scattered on the ground in restricted grid patterns. The one town where one might hope and expect to find some indication or reflection of the new Israeli society turns out to be a characterless and featureless extension in concrete, a wilful tiny Los Angeles. The new rich, most of the five hundred acknowledged millionaires, have come in on the land boom, and their exploitation of the economic and real-estate factors which govern the urgent housing problem has negated the attempt to create something organic, a town of people gathered for communal purposes.

The old Neve Tsedek quarter, where the first settlers moved out of Jaffa, is now a quiet slum, its big, once prosperous houses sinking into accepted abandon. Nothing has been modernized or repainted for years. Only a few survivors remain, misfits, the poor and illiterate, those unable to get out. The bare, abandoned site of the former Jaffa-Petah Tikvah railway line cuts through the quarter, its embankment piled high with debris. Ruined warehouses loom behind the old track: a few old watchmen read or sleep on their wicker chairs in the sun. The area has been rejected and presumably is now ready for development. Yet in itself the district is unique, full of tall-porticoed Middle East Edwardian houses with colonnades and caryatids. There is plenty of detail worth preserving, carved lintels, balconies whose roundels are adorned with the star of David; courtyards covered by glass and ironwork and shaded by vines. Historically this was the nucleus of the old town, a hybrid mixture of Pressburg and Damascus in conception. The process of spiralling away to the newest suburbs of the city is self-perpetuating, so the city spreads northwards, artificially creating a slum wake in what should be its organic centre. No sooner is the claim staked, as it were, than the gold-rush is off in another direction. Fashion begins to have some control: districts are now not smart, belonging to last year, or to the year before. The culmination of this is the removal of those elements with money to Herzlia or Ramat Gan, bringing into existence a commuter class which streams in to work along roads never conceived for such purposes. A few miles outside Tel Aviv, the only stretch of dual carriageway comes to a halt. Los Angeles is nearer than ever. The city visually most similar to Tel Aviv, however, lies a few hours' drive up the coast. Beirut has also suffered from the same hasty modernization: ugly little blocks intersperse the fashionable modernity of the luxury hotels and flats rising slab upon slab. There is the same atmosphere of suspended bustle and unfinishing enterprise, with the same unco-ordinated results. Walking around Beirut is almost hallucinatory to someone familiar with Tel Aviv.

The old structure is challenged fundamentally by the money which is to be made in the general expansion. Acquisition in Haifa is a tacit criterion of status: in Tel Aviv it is an awkward subject of conversation. The role of money in such a changing society may be beneficial, and there are plenty of apologists, some less uneasy than others about the new-found affluence. But there are as many who have inherited the widespread belief—a legacy from their nineteenth-century socialist forebears for whom progress involved strong self-denial and deliberate puritanism—that the life of a city is incompatible with clean or decent existence. Yet this is the world they have grown up in and with which they have to be reconciled.

Against this grows the boss complex, a sure way of naturally inhibiting freedom of choice, but one only natural in a society still open enough to allow overriding personal ambitions. Activity commands respect. Stratification follows, especially since the ambitious have by and large acquired their skills and values in Western society. Young men in shiny tropical suits proliferate, talking patronizingly and deprecatingly about the country and the crying need for a good managerial class. They drive big cars and give cocktail parties for fellow executives, earnest, studious, well-informed, able to prove in a few sentences the wastage and the inefficiency of a kibbutz.

Their parents on the other hand are usually part of the large amorphous *bourgeoisie* of Tel Aviv, living at a more restrained tempo. The elder generation seems taken aback by this positive, materialistic efflorescence and is quietly critical. It is as if so much has been achieved during their lifetime that they can afford to sit on the balcony playing cards with their friends and accept what has miraculously grown up around them. They can rest on their laurels. Indulgence was a liberty hitherto impermissible. If the young want to indulge themselves now, it doesn't really matter how they do it. Careerism is as much a novelty as anything else. Against such attitudes, politicians and the young appear immensely conspicuous as they juggle in their different ways with the old structure—and slightly ridiculous in their attitudes of self-importance.

Protest at the adulteration of socialist values is limited to very small groups. In an expanding society, carping is bound to take place on the sidelines. Here are not the self-conscious intellectual communities of European cities, but instead isolated individuals—journalists, scientists, civil servants, prepared to be highly critical in the seclusion of their apartments. The main debate is about the state of Israeli society which is bound up with Israel's place in the Middle East. On the whole, these men's opinions lie outside the framework of party politics, which is treated rather as a natural preserve where certain creatures like to sport and know they will be watched. With careers of every kind open to talent, the number and status of those in the political preserves tend to diminish. The elder generation in turn, hearing arguments about socialist values, often dismiss them as typical examples of the Jewish conscience at work, while paying lip-service to these values which they believe are being put into practice. The immediate Israeli context is satisfying enough and analytical criticism therefore must have its origins in guilt. This dead emotion, they can imply, is being artificially revived.

Kibbutzniks can be spotted a mile off in Tel Aviv, with their drab clothes and their air of fascinated incredulity. 'Isn't it dreadful, all these people running about and doing nothing?' We were walking down Dizengoff and a *kibbutznik* friend began to spell out what a difference it would make if he could conscript the café loungers for two weeks, or four, and how much good it would do them if their indolence and indecision were replaced by some useful farm

work. It was distasteful to him to sit at one of the tables
reaching over the pavement, and he began to complain of
the petrol fumes from the street, of the unpleasantness of
travelling by bus, of the headache which he suffered when
he entered a city. For him, this holiday in Tel Aviv was a
penance.

To be accused of loitering in Dizengoff cafés means to
belong to the new undecided generation. There are those
who free themselves by publicly denouncing café values and
setting off on some daring enterprise such as founding a
co-operative town in the Negev. There are also a few with
equal single-mindedness, who determinedly keep on dancing the twist in one of the humid cellars which have appeared
almost overnight. The young have been caught between
conflicting values and have nowhere to turn to resolve
them. The cinema has become the social occasion *par
excellence*, for the regular viewing of the latest, but by no
means the best, films from France and Italy. Only the oldest
cinema in Tel Aviv, the Eden, a fantasticated piece of architecture in the Neve Tsedek, provides an exception in the
Arab films which it shows, most of them lush parodies of
Western romances. The sidewalks are the social parade.
There are a few strip joints, and at the famous Mograbi one
finds a hypnotist most of the time. Late at night couples
crowd on to the beach, singing, eating, lovemaking. Sometimes a brawl starts up with the inhabitants of the *maabaroth*
—the temporary huts which still huddle on the beach, an
ugly fringe to the luxury hotels.

More exclusive is the Bohemian world of artists, living
largely in Jaffa and taking its cosmopolitanism for granted.
'We're not wearing beards this year—they aren't in Paris.'
Jaffa has elements of a mock St Tropez, where the artists
have settled, set up galleries and decorated chi-chi night
clubs. In a converted Turkish bath, a revue spoofs the early
Tel Aviv pioneers, patronizing but not unkind. Pioneering
is for the music-hall. The few Bohemians have an influence
disproportionate to their numbers. Clustered in one or two

cafés, they are an attraction for passers-by unused to such blasé idleness. Behind the shore, however, with its pretty studios and garrets, stretch the one- or two-room slum houses, as full of children as of chickens. Food in the little booths is dirty: apathetic hawkers stare. Garbage trickles down the cobbled gutter in the middle of the street, and the smells are acrid. Here, work is chancy, living conditions hazardous. There is no integration with Israeli society. Most of the former population has disappeared, so that the present inhabitants are either the poorest Arabs who remained or casual labourers in the building trades or restaurant workers who cannot find a bed in Tel Aviv or could not afford to pay for one. Almost indistinguishable from them are the North Africans, who provide the Arabs with their daily contact with Jewish life: the traditional circumstances of the Middle East have survived here. There are a few craftsmen and artisans plying their trade in the market which is still much like the old Arab bazaar, although the merchandise is inevitably of worse quality now that Jaffa has lost its importance as a clearing-port for Arab trade. Disappointment and discontent rumble underneath. Once I said to a workman there that I liked coming to Jaffa. He wrinkled up his nose and spread out his hands disdainfully. Then he spat on the floor.

At present, Manchia, the ground between Jaffa and Tel Aviv, is still lying waste, devastated by the war. It is the last part of the town which could be developed as a park, as a distinctive centre for the city, giving some cohesion to the different elements. This project has been rejected and instead the land has been handed over to private British capital to exploit by raising a complex of banks, offices and stock-exchange. Out of the present chaotic jumble of Tel Aviv anything, however auto-destructive, can emerge: Arthur Koestler described it as 'a frantic, touching, maddening city which gripped the traveller by the buttonhole'. The traveller must equally grip back: a free-for-all is on and somebody might get strangled by mistake. The usual judgements get polarized: positive means doing something; criticism is negative. On the positive side, there are the neat, planned and successful workers' houses on the outskirts of Tel Aviv, beyond the industrial quarters around Rehov Giborey Yisrael. Those who occupy this housing know what they have got and are satisfied, for the refrigerator, the new furniture, the cheap paperbacks, provide an initial security and comfort which makes most of these estates rather like separately developed little communities, almost urban kibbutzim. At this level social integration is a reality, and this is perhaps the foundation which will enable a new tradition to evolve. Somewhere a synthesis has to be achieved, or the melting-pot will itself melt away or turn into a Levantine hodge-podge. The latter is already a much feared, and therefore much publicized, threat. All things are possible: work seems like endeavour: this is the buoyant feeling sustaining Tel Aviv. It also creates the important new standards of personal success and failure. A sense of purpose becomes confused with a spirit of competition: communal identity and capitalist enterprise go uneasily hand in hand. Yet somehow the rigid figures of the pioneers in the snapshots need modernizing, but not by being ignored, or caricatured in a theatrical turn. The new images of material progress and bourgeois sophistication have got to enter in.

I spent some time wandering around Tel Aviv with a friend who wanted to show me what it had been like to grow up there. When we tried to find our way through some of the streets he got lost, for they had been changed out of all recognition. He began complaining of the lack of tradition, that the whole character of the place had been expunged until there was nothing which might give pleasure or offence. He found his way by noticing some tile mosaics on the upper storey of a house, depicting Zionist virtues stylized in agricultural postures. It would have given the designer some pleasure that anyone was still aware of the existence of these ugly pre-Raphaelitish tiles, for they were hard to spot from ground level, obscured behind trees and partially concealed by billboards backing advertising signs.

III

The important question of organic growth comes to a head in Jerusalem. The quick industrial upheaval of Haifa has been a race which has left the runners gasping for breath and looking back over their shoulders. Tel Aviv is a twentieth-century parable, falling back for its own consolidation on to its parents and instead exacting a toll from its children. Jerusalem, in spite of the ups and downs of its history, has grown into its present condition by means of recognizable and deliberate actions for which the agents at least found natural justifications. This is not simply to say that it is the oldest or the most unspoilt or the most historical of the three towns. Jerusalem has felt the same social pressures, the same tensions, the same necessities, and it suffered the worst fate in the War of Independence by being shorn away from the Old City, geographically separated from most of what was traditionally important to its continuous existence. Also the buildings in the New City, with few exceptions, only delude the visitor with a sense of antiquity; there is hardly anything here older than in Tel Aviv, except the name. The showplaces are either hindsight reconstructions with little or no archaeological authority, or—like the Tower of David and indeed much else in the Old City—minor Turkish fortifications which have served to catch legends. In Old and New Jerusalem mythomania grips guide and tourist alike, for credulity is the common currency. Moreover, whatever Jerusalem may have meant imaginatively, spiritually or intellectually, in practice it was always a disparate set of communities, hardly an entity. In many ways this still applies, for important distinctions of habits and language divide the German quarter from the Bokharian, or the Anglo-Saxon from the Hungarian.

Everything should have combined, it might be supposed, to destroy the character of Jerusalem. First the influx of soldiers during the second world war, then the siege and the ensuing partition, the loss of Mount Scopus and its university, the establishment of government, and finally the over-spilling population, resulting here as elsewhere in the necessary building of housing estates without regard to landscape, and most particularly evident and painful in the Judean hills, without the use of stone; that ripe-coloured stone which so enhances the gaunt surroundings. Yet in a way difficult to define, the events have been accretions, adapting and transforming what was there before but adding in the process. The distance between the old and the new does not matter a great deal: there remains an identifiable thread somewhere which gives the inhabitants a sense of natural continuity and identity. Of course Jerusalem has the advantage of its complex associations, but in the housing developments which climb up the stony brown hills, life is not much different in quality from life in any other such developments. There is just an imponderable balance—metaphysical if you will—between living in a city like Haifa or Tel Aviv, devised on some fortuitously vacant location and approved by a bureaucracy with its planning needs and quotas, and living in a place which has a *raison d'être*, however varied and diffuse and changeable. It proves an over-riding consideration. By far the most stable and self-confident element in Israeli society is to be found in the rural settlements, kibbutz or *moshav*, which have a comparatively new tradition but one sufficiently identifiable and vigorous to sustain them and provide a steady orientation in so fluid a realignment of population. There is no such reference in urban life. Only Jerusalem, of the three big cities, seems to provide something similar, some framework which obviates the question nobody wants to ask: 'What am I doing here?'

In itself Jerusalem is quite dull. One long busy thorough-fare, small bazaar-like shops, a few cinemas, but no theatre or real community centre. Its attractions are staid, the museums, memorials, the scenery, the sparse antiquities, a permanent exhibition about the country, some conventional municipal statuary. Official buildings multiply. Most of the large central blocks now under construction are unimaginative government offices. Then there are the Christian monasteries or churches, drawing attention to themselves by their state of disrepair and neglect, like blotches of blight or mildew in the active atmosphere. The seventeenth-century monastery in the Valley of the Cross appears permanently closed: a ramshackle Russian orthodox monastery is now a police station: the convent of Notre Dame de Sion offers a wonderful view of the Old City as the culmination of a long climb up its flights of cracked stone stairs so dingy and deserted that a footstep echoes like a gunshot. One whole wing sags from its wartime bombardment, and it is still propped around with sandbags. Only the YMCA, big and yellow and flatulent, offers the attractions of its swimming pool and its extra-mural studies, to give the impression of participation in the daily life. The church of the Dormition, uneasy in no-man's-land, and hedged off with barbed wire behind its Germano-Byzantine solidity, fulfils the original glistening intentions of its founders. Alongside is the second-floor Crusader-vaulted room which passes for the scene of the Last Supper, but otherwise there is little for the tourist or the pilgrim.

Whereas in Tel Aviv communal bustle tends to empty people into the streets, in Jerusalem its absence confines them to their homes. The official receptions and cocktail parties and tours for visiting delegations furnish the exceptional occasions for ceremonies which tend to be announced to the public at the moment by the quick turnover of blue and white *Vive-le-Président* strip-banners across the main road, in honour of yet one more head of state. Otherwise Jerusalem seems a city of domestic virtue, epitomized by the peaceful districts of Katamon, Rehavia, Talpioth or Beth Hakerem. There is less here of the steady card-playing spun out with balcony talk included in Tel Aviv's desultory routine, more watering of gardens, walking to vantage points to admire the Old City or distant Bethlehem, concentration on work, on reading, on family circles. Just as a *moshav* is designed for a family unit, so is Jerusalem. It is not a place in which to be single. The tempo is *andante*.

The reflection, indeed the resumé of this, is to be seen in the university and its students. Principally occupying the area of Givat Ram and expanding fast, but also spread about the town in various subsidiary centres, the university naturally exerts a considerable influence on the life of Jerusalem, perhaps more extensively than the wide but continuous government business. Student accommodation is hard to find, and a high proportion of students are scattered around the town in hired rooms. They live a very free life, bound only by the exigencies of their university programme. Since there are few distractions, and few student activities as such, the conditions for study are favourable. Only rarely do students stage a play or give a concert, and there is no outlet for journalism. In the students' hostel where I stayed, it was generally accepted as a result that at nine in the evening one sat down for three or four hours' work, irrespective of how heavy the day's programme had been.

Accompanying this intensity was an attitude towards the work itself. It was not seen as a training of the mind, as a suitable basis for some future but unspecified task. Rather it was straightforward acquisition of knowledge, of facts and authoritative opinions for direct utilitarian purposes. For someone like myself from an English university, the absence of theorizing was novel. I tried to explain this to my roommate, a *sabra* doing graduate research in organic chemistry. It seemed incomprehensible to him that students might learn anything by discussion and attempts to refute their tutors' lectures. Questions of right and wrong were immaterial: that would come later when one had acquired as much knowledge as one's elders. Until then one's opinion was inadequate and talking rubbish was the mark of the idle student. It was necessary, he said, to be a jackdaw before one could evolve into an eagle. When I explained that an Oxford student might attend lectures contingent or irrelevant to his subject, just to acquire often hypothetical arguments, he became stern. Although serious and dismayed by Oxford wastage, he was far from priggish, but merely ignored anything outside his field, on the basis of some private equation of matter to be absorbed and time available. On this principle he sometimes read a Peter Cheyney thriller or a war story for weekend relaxation.

Compared to an English university where neurosis spreads like seaweed, clamping on to a student's energies, this matter-of-fact attitude gives the university life a secure foundation and points a change from the older tradition of acquiring knowledge for knowledge's sake, a luxury scarcely obtainable or permissible in this context. There were, it is true, students less intensive about their work, who sat around in their lodgings playing gramophone records, going dancing, rushing off to Tel Aviv or to the seaside on scooters. But they seemed exceptional, coming usually from the small section of students with money. In their economics and administration courses, moreover, they assiduously prepared for careers as bankers and businessmen.

Practical considerations hold also so far as the Arab students are concerned. Arabs in Haifa are by and large a rump group left over from the exodus: in Tel Aviv they are a rarity except in various menial occupations. Admittedly the number of Arab students at the university of Jerusalem is small—less than one hundred. But they are serious and industrious and treated accordingly. I was taken aside by one, a graduate medical student, and asked to be lenient in judging what he called the childishness of his friends. It came from a lack of *savoir-faire*, he explained. We had been discussing the film *Exodus*, a film which was currently showing in the city and of which he and his friends disapproved for its historical peculiarities which they took to provide a vicious anti-Arab bias. They objected to the presentation of historical episodes in travestied but recognisable form, under the guise of fiction. Nothing, they said, could be gained by superimposing distortions on a situation already prone to

33

fantasy. But the question which chiefly preoccupied them was the Arab students' perennial bugbear: what job to get afterwards? The harder it becomes for them to obtain the work for which their training has equipped them, clearly the more a discontented Arab intelligentsia is likely to develop. As in other contexts in Jerusalem, enthusiasm to work overshadowed other considerations for the Arabs, even if this should prove only temporary.

There are other minorities in Jerusalem which call for pragmatic approaches. It is impossible to live here, for however short a time, without facing the religious conflicts. Sabbath in Jerusalem has the distinctive, bleak and humanly forsaken qualities of a Welsh or Scottish Sunday. If the weather is hot, long queues stand at the head of the main road out, importuning passing cars in the absence of public transport, sometimes waiting half a day in vain for a lift. Yet the newly formed League for the Prevention of Religious Coercion finds little support. When the League ran buses out to the Hadassah Hospital over a trial period, there was little popular approval, nor much advantage taken of the service. Even the kibbutzim which had provided the transport felt uneasy about their connivance. The religious extremists make their influence felt at all levels of daily life, not only politically through the complicated coalition which allows them to barter votes for concessions, but in their everyday contacts and continuous encroachments on other citizens' liberties. Everybody is familiar with the opinions of the handful of the *Neturei Karta*—the sect which believes that the state of Israel is blasphemous, for only the Messiah can bring it about—and differentiates between them and the lesser fanaticisms, although perhaps a subject such as Israeli foreign policy would not produce any such informed arguments. For the highly opinionated dogmas of the extremists are treated half as exoticisms and half as a spiritual heritage worthy of understanding and, sometimes, of reluctant admiration. The central attitude lies somewhere within this ambivalence, for what potentially could be an irreconcilable clash has become café talk. A woman will be hissed for wearing short sleeves in certain areas of the city, or a car will be stoned on the Sabbath—the extremists have their way in matters touching anywhere on religion. But they have had to pay the price of intolerance in their isolation. Mea Shearim, accordingly, is half a tourist attraction and half an asset, a thing which is quite interesting and even pleasant to have around because it adds another dimension to life. There are a few inconveniences, but these are quite easy to shrug off; and meanwhile there is work to be done which cannot be hampered by any intractable religious considerations. Mea Shearim slowly shrinks into itself, recorded by the tourists' cameras.

Everything in Jerusalem, Mea Shearim included for it is right against the border, is drawn closer by the wall, with its single aperture at the Mandelbaum Gate opening into the Arab countries although only for a trip in one direction. Unexpectedly, the wall rises round the street corners, a thin, high, ugly strip of discoloured concrete, cutting through blocks of war-damaged and abandoned houses. In places the wall is hardly more than a token division, for the Jordanian sentry-post will look down from a sandbagged crow's-nest just behind it, or conversations are exchanged good-naturedly from balcony to balcony. Most of the views in Jerusalem, from whatever vantage points, are towards the Old City and its encompassing hills, across no-man's-land, with the wall somewhere below one's feet. As in West Berlin, fortressed even more obstructively, the wall and the troops patrolling give a sense of identity, an almost medieval feeling of living within manned battlements, shuttered against immediate hostile forces. But unlike West Berlin, the identity produced is not highly-strung but self-reliant. One afternoon I happened to be on a rooftop looking towards the Old City, trying to locate the Victorian gothic cloisters of the Anglican St George's Hostel where I would be staying some weeks later, when a fatal shooting occurred in the streets of Musrara not far below me. An old man and his daughter had been fired upon—one of a number of such incidents that summer. It was all over and done with in two minutes. The only repercussion seemed to come from a party of French tourists who felt themselves directly threatened, and cowered where they were, as if still in danger, for a long time afterwards. By chance I ran into them again the following day at the university, and they were still complaining of the ordeal. But to their Jerusalem audience, it was a matter of past history.

Behind the wall, inside the university, around its traditions, somehow Jerusalem has fused together into an integrated city. Perhaps it is due to the associations of its name; or the tolerance of its elder generation, the Bubers and the Agnons, now Grand Old Men who have grown to stature in these surroundings; or, simply as the seat of government. Rooted in the past, it is prepared for Israel's future in some purposeful way not reciprocated in Tel Aviv or Haifa which are far more modern cities in many, perhaps more essential, ways. It does not mean that life in Jerusalem is pleasanter or more interesting, more cultivated or more self-conscious than elsewhere. On the whole it is probably none of these things, and many details of daily life are naturally common to the three large cities of modern Israel. Characteristics which can be defined as specifically Israeli are being evolved at a different pace in different parts of the country. Many of these attitudes of mind and ways of behaving have grown out of what preceded them, yet nevertheless exist essentially in their own right, created by the circumstances in which they were generated. This welding process is too large and diffuse to have any uniformity: the finished product depends upon the handicraft of many welders working in isolation from one another. The contrast between the three cities, then, is one of pace, but this pace will have to be stabilized before the tenor of Israeli life is finally established.

Chapter Two

ADA

I HAD BEEN GIVEN a letter to Ada. It was unsealed so naturally I had read it. He is a talkative Englishman, it said, and that ought to entertain you: please be kind to him. I licked the envelope, because it was too unflattering to have such an open witness. The letter had been written for me by someone whom I did not know well, and I could accept it as a sign of politeness, and stuffed it into my suitcase. But when I found myself living in Ruppin Street I remembered Ada's address. She was only three houses away.

Tel Aviv is not an easy city to enter. The first time I drove in under the blue-and-white triumphal arch with its painted Welcome, I went on and on through an expanse of industrial suburb to another blue-and-white Farewell arch. There is no indication which of the three or four long streets leads to the sea, and there is no horizon of blue to act as a pointer: the city is a knotted backbone with no ribs. Ruppin Street, which I was trying to find, is in the centre of the maze, after long burrowings and blocked streets at right angles; yet it is also only a short walk from the shore. The smaller the streets, the more the trees overhang the pavements, and Ruppin Street is improbably shaded: a sanctuary in the maze.

I was living in a skyscraper which abutted on to Ruppin Street. For the moment it is the tallest building in Tel Aviv, its eight stories rising above the ground-floor supermarket. From its flats there is the best view in Tel Aviv of the long,

stringent coast, while inland lies the jumbled townscape in
its uniform range of colours—grey, brown and yellow—
as if baked by the climate, all huddled into the thin bottleneck of land between the sea and the Jordanian boundary
which runs along the foothills in the middle distance. From
my room too, I could look down into the houses opposite
and watch what was going on, and as I later discovered, I
could almost see into Ada's flat.

I was busy for some time after I had settled into the skyscraper, and I delayed going to call, but I did push the letter
under her door with a scribbled sentence on it that I was
now her neighbour, without saying where. Later she would
refer to this, calling it an example of typical English
behaviour. But one morning in the supermarket a little,
elderly woman stopped me. She had a very thin face, bony
and elongated, with frizzy, grey hair. Ada had deduced who
I was because she knew every other person regularly
shopping at eleven-thirty in the supermarket. With small,
fast swoops, she filled up her trolley and then made me carry
her goods home. As we walked into the three-storied
building where she lived I noticed that she was the only
inhabitant not to put the Hebrew version of her name on her
post-box in the entrance, not even to make the concession of
having her name in the two alphabets, but sticking rigidly
to the Latin characters.

Her flat was an assortment of untidiness. Three, or as the
Israeli house-agents say, three and a half cramped rooms; a
short verandah giving on to the sheer concrete surface of a
hotel side-wall opposite; an entrance hall thinned to a
passage with books heaped on top of each other—Ada lived
like a ferret within these limits. Sometimes it seemed that
she had designed the obstructions: an upright piano almost
blocked the door of her sitting room, but being so thin and
shrunken herself, she never appeared to notice how incon-
venient it was for others to enter the room, pressing the
jutting-out keyboard into their stomach. On the walls were
reproductions of seventeenth-century prints of the *Terra*

Sancta; maps of the holy places with specious, silvery apologies in Latin to account for the Turkish occupation. The rooms were altogether rather more like an old bachelor's.

While I was made to sit down, Ada disappeared into the kitchen and noisily began making coffee, throwing questions down the passage. What was I doing in Israel? Did I find Jews ugly? The hero of Arthur Koestler's novel couldn't bear to look at Israelis because of their ugliness—had I seen the glass museum, the only thing of any taste in the country? What did I think about circumcision? Like all compulsive talkers, Ada never wanted an answer but was merely releasing balloons which were not to be recaptured. Coffee eventually appeared, but she had burnt it and then slopped it all over her brass tray. We talked about our mutual acquaintance, until she asked me what I thought I was going to find in Israel. She came back to this question, cocking her head to one side like an intelligent bird. 'You must have got a prepared answer, you've been here long enough, and I don't want to hear that.' Suddenly, after the barrage, she decided that it was time for lunch, and in honour of our meeting in the supermarket, we would go out to her favourite restaurant. This turned out to be a long way from Ruppin Street, along the seafront, and all she wanted was a particular kind of *hors d'oeuvre* which it took her about fifteen minutes to eat and then, with the last gherkin in her mouth, she was off. She explained that she had to go and work; her job was to translate and also to digest German newspapers and magazines and she also translated from the Russian. Before I could stop her, she had paid the bill and flitted off through the revolving door and down the esplanade.

For someone whose announced function was to talk to Ada, I never found much opportunity to perform. I was incorporated into her life, much as she digested her daily German newspaper articles, in an automatic process of ingression, which she began later in the week by taking me to see her niece who was married to a journalist on the evening paper and lived in a new suburb at Bat Yam. Tel Aviv plays leapfrog over the Arab town of Jaffa, which is now encrusted between the sprawling modern suburbs which spread with baffling uniformity. Ada took every wrong turn. We often found ourselves driving over dunes after the tarmac had given out into sand: 'Now I know where we are.' There was a low shed thrown together by the side of the road. Triumphantly Ada pointed to the home of Yemeni handcrafts. 'You'll love the weaving, I know you don't want to go in, but I support them so you must.' It was no good protesting that she had brought me there under false pretences. Inside, fifteen women were working at rugs or embroidering hand-made dresses and scarves. Ada was slightly ashamed at having taken me and therefore was all the more insistent that I should see everything, that all the cloth should be taken down from the shelves and unwrapped, that I should have it explained meticulously why the skills of the Yemeni women should be preserved. The hut was low, airless and smelly with the acridity of too many stale wools and stuffs and cottons, and the Yemeni women looked at us with modest but unflinching eyes. Ada busied us off to her niece.

On the way I first discovered her high hatred of the Germans. It was the real emotion of hate, refined and sad in its intensity. She had begun to tell me of a dinner party where she had met Thomas Mann, 'the proper German spirit'. The little brick buildings outside retreated across the sandhills: the housing estates grew up in compressed anonymity: and as the landscape went past, she told me that Thomas Mann had not understood some joke she had made, he was a person with little sense of humour. She repeated the story to her niece, shortly after we had arrived, but the niece could not speak a word of German and it was lost on her. Ada went on to maintain that the Germans were inherently cruel and vicious and stupid as a race, and that her niece was quite right not to learn their language. Sadism was a racial characteristic of the Germans and one had to accept it, but the niece, who had plainly heard this before, started to explain patiently that other nations had behaved in the same calculatedly monstrous way—not that the behaviour was thereby mitigated—but this was proof that cruelty was something universal. Ada's face became pure with hate—the lines and crooked features were smoothed out, but there was nothing hysterical in her feelings, only a secure conviction. To her, racialism was a fact and always would be, and for these reasons she would never accept a penny of the German reparations which she could have received. Acceptance of the money would be hypocrisy for her; it would negate the facts.

They argued about these German reparations, for the niece thought that the Germans honestly wanted to make amends even if, in the nature of things, the amends would only be in the distasteful form of money. Ada firmly held that suffering and murder were not to be paid for in this way, that they could be expiated. 'I'm not part of your new civilisation of weights and measures,' I remember her saying, 'I'm going to be old-fashioned and use the standards of what one can do and what one can't. *Das tut sich nicht.*' She turned to me for support. 'But like that one would never forget anything, let alone forgive,' interrupted the niece, and Ada answered that this was the real merit of her doctrine, it was historical. Nobody ever forgets a bad turn— schoolchildren are educated on lists of massacres. Israel too had grown up like that, and Ada did not want them to over- look it: she found it squeamish to bury one's head in the eastern shore of the Mediterranean and then be paid for the pleasure of having sand in the eyes. Israelis, just like Jews, ought to accept the fact that other people don't like them and have paid them to stay out of the way.

But her niece was too phlegmatic to be aroused, and also discounted most of what Ada was saying as the guilt and the remaining fear of an elder European generation. With a sluggish smile, she left the room to prepare tea. Behind her back, Ada was scornful about her. 'Such rubbish, like all explanations of human wickedness. We just aren't all alike. But she's a typical young Israeli who can't understand the dimensions of such a catastrophe, she's dismissed the catastrophe, not her failure to understand. It's natural if you didn't live through it. If she has any villains, it is a lot of knobbly-kneed young English soldiers who couldn't tell a Jew from an Arab and wished all of them in hell. Or she has nightmares about ill-shaven, dirty Arabs coming to rape her—as if that's what they want to do. The wretched thing is that this a case where forgiving is bound up with living in a foreign country.'

Tea and a large creamy cake pacified her. The niece managed to tell me in the interludes that really she thought Ada a wonderful old woman after all she had been through, and one had to make every allowance—Europe and her house and her friends had been everything to her—and she ought to take the money and make herself comfortable.

Evening was coming on; the sudden dark blanket of the Mediterranean, spreading immediately after the sun disappears below the horizon with the semblance of a tiny flash. Ada wanted to leave. Her journalist nephew had still not come home, but Ada's patience could not wait on politeness, and the conversation had induced a state of nervousness. All the way back to Tel Aviv, through the traffic and the headlights and the darkness which was a compound of resinous smells and petrol, Ada talked of the Vienna of her childhood, of her father's friends, the professors and the writers, of Schoenberg's quarter and her piano lessons from the great man. I hardly had the courage to ask her any questions, because this past had plainly just been evoked by her niece's insensitivity, but I listened to what she had to say in the bustle of rush-hour as the cars thronged the narrow roads. When I dropped her home after this turmoil, Ruppin Street seemed even more of a haven.

Sometimes I used to call on her after this visit, late in the evenings during the summer. We would sit on her verandah, hoping to catch any cool breeze from the sea, under an awning which kept off the humidity gathering like dew. A small circle of her friends was usually to be found there: a man who kept a secondhand book shop and who was fortunate enough to visit Europe for his stock; one or two writers, including a histrionic poet who would suddenly stand up and declaim his verse in a rather Slav manner; a few elderly ladies in dresses of a nondescript, timeless fashion with big beads thumping round their necks. If the evening was too damp and sticky for much talk, or the poet had brought all conversation to an end with a recital, Ada could be persuaded to play her piano. It had not been tuned for most of its long life and all the notes had the plangent pitch of a mandolin—there was no point tuning it in such a climate, for the strings slackened at once. Its keys had dulled to a lemon-brown which contrasted oddly with Ada's bony white fingers and neat nails, but in spite of all the disadvantages she would sit down as if she were giving a concert performance. Schumann, Chopin, Liszt—the piano melted them into a sweet, thin soup. It suited exactly the mood of those evenings, the almost Russian intensity of the crowded room, the poet's stricken profile and the old women's stately melancholy. Once Ada must have been a capable pianist—all expression and inflection. She knew too that she was casting a spell over us all, immobilizing us on those turgid summer nights, the romantic incantations fixing us to our chairs with only a hand free to stretch out for a fresh date or a glass of fruit juice. Ruppin Street was always very quiet at night, as if the neighbours stayed cooped in their flats. It was surprising that they never complained because without Ada's presence to enhance it the music must have sounded quite painful.

Once, after such an evening when Ada had stayed up late playing some Chopin, I left the flat with the poet. We walked down the wide Ben Yehuda Street past the supermarket and along to a night club which the poet thought would be a fitting end to the evening. He did not want to go to a café in case he should meet all the other poets—the Slonskys and the Altermanns—whom there would be no avoiding. We went down into an underground cellar, the Key Club, where there was a big twist session going on, in spite of the stifling heat. Around us were the universal pink lights and the bar decorations and the young serious faces: we could hardly hear ourselves speak for the blare of the radiogram. He wanted to talk intensely: what did I think of Tel Aviv? Whom had I met? Did I know Max Brod, the editor and friend of Kafka? I steered him on to the subject of Ada, but at first he was unwilling to talk about her. Yet it was apparent that she filled some important part of his life which was otherwise missing. He thought that she represented a side of Israeli life which I shouldn't really have seen—the old and the sad and the failed. 'She's wonderfully brave though, and after all she's been through, she's got the right to be a bit of a *poseuse*; and I admire her for it.' After some whisky he became silent and nostalgic, sometimes uttering broody remarks about Prague before the war, and the old friends: 'but you wouldn't know what I mean.' The young girls and boys were twisting—their bodies mobile with rhythm. He tried to explain how he admired Ada for refusing to take the money which the Germans offered as reparations. 'We had standards which these don't know about,' and he indicated the dancers. After a pause he recovered himself—with a little more to drink—and we were on to Kafka again. He promised that I should not leave Tel Aviv without being introduced to Max Brod, to what was left of the 'old world'. The dancing was still going on when we finally left, to emerge into the sultry street.

In order to repay some of my obligations to Ada, I bought tickets for a concert of Viennese music, and I was glad to see that the idea pleased her. In a way too, it was a farewell to Ruppin Street because the flat was to be handed back to its owners shortly and I would be leaving Tel Aviv to return to Haifa. Perhaps Ada had realized what this occasion might represent, or perhaps it was just anticipation of the concert, but at any rate she had put on a blue evening dress which trailed around her ankles and an antique fox fur. The humidity, even at night, made a tie feel like a noose, but Ada was never a person to pay attention to such external inconveniences as the climate. Round her neck dangled a string of fat, artificial pearls and she was carrying a minute embroidered evening bag. She might have been going to the Vienna opera shortly after the first world war.

Nor was the music very different from the kind of thing she would have heard in a concert at that date. The first part consisted of a Beethoven symphony and some Schubert, while the second half was unashamedly Strauss. German was the language of the audience but Viennese their sentiments— the music had been especially provided for them, and one could feel them responding as waltz gaily rounded into waltz or straightened into a march. Ada was dressed quite correctly, fitting unobtrusively into the crowd. In my white shirt with sleeves rolled up, it was I who was conspicuous, all the more so as the Liberian president was an official guest and Tel Aviv's largest auditorium, the Frederic Mann hall, was packed as a consequence with formally dressed people. During the interval, Ada took me round the auditorium, showing me the permanent exhibits to the memory of Bronislaw Hubermann, the violinist, who had been a friend of hers, and she launched into anecdotes about him and Toscanini and the foundation of the Israel Philharmonic Orchestra. Many of her friends had been helped out of Europe in that way. After the concert, too, Ada was excited and in no mood to go home. Infected with the nostalgia of the final bouncy waltz tunes, she continued telling stories about past performances she had heard. When we got back to the car, she asked if we could go for a short drive so that she could get her breath back. She wanted to drive along the coast, and so I went along Arlosoroff towards the blue-and-white Welcome arch and on to the dual carriageway running up the coast. It was a wonderfully clear night, in spite of the mugginess which condenses on to everything, even needing wipers to clean it off the windscreen. Once out of Tel Aviv the road was virtually empty, and I drove a few miles as far as the village suburb of Herzlia, where there is the first accessible and clean stretch of sandy shore. Turning down a side road under an avenue of sturdy trees, I decided to go towards the deserted part of the beach. Off the tarmac, we bumped along a sandy track, through a district of jerry-built shacks and huts for poor immigrants, towards a headland. On the open ground was spread a former British army camp, the barrack huts desolate and white among wiry heather. It had been a radar station for spotting ships illegally running the blockade in the closing months of the Mandate. Israeli soldiers seemed to have taken it over, but the place looked more or less deserted: it might have been a holiday camp out of season.

I parked the car at the end of the track, next to one of the disused and padlocked military huts. A single palm tree stood up on the skyline, breaking the flat surface of the head-land and the sea below. Ada wanted to walk down the short path to the sea, across an unkempt and sandy waste which had been scattered with rubbish and bits of scrap. Her old-fashioned button shoes and long dress were supremely inappropriate but she set off, fastidiously picking her way, stepping over the litter left by picnickers or overspilling from the immigrants' huts now blackened into the shadows of their little gardens. Out of the night came the distant noise of Arab music. Opposite the barracks, as if to balance it on a matching cliff, but slightly set back, was a squat mosque, with a thick and rather awkward minaret parallel to the square tower of the Mandate radar station. Attached to the mosque was a former religious school, with its cells round an enclosed courtyard. But it had been badly damaged in the fighting and was now closed off and locked. The Palmach had painted their mark above the entrance to com-memorate the soldiers who had captured the place, and the whole wall now gleamed white as it caught the moonlight. The path to the sea lay down a sloping cleft between these two rising promontories crowned with mosque and barracks, where I caught up with Ada to take her arm and we climbed down the curving path to the shore.

The sand was packed hard and we walked along its edge with the waves splashing in a few yards off, only to seep obsequiously towards the land. Far in the distance the lights of Tel Aviv glowed a dullish orange, filtered through the darkness. In front of us the beach thinned away, a dwindling bright thread at the foot of the rock which rose abruptly like an escarpment from the sand. Voices came from somewhere above the cliff. Another and steeper path led down to the small inlet which we had reached. Some people had been bathing: soldiers from the barracks perhaps. Out of the water rose chunks of solid masonry, black but gleaming as the waves broke against them, sending froth to bubble against the jetty of a narrow harbour. These were the ramparts of the Roman harbour of Apollonia, long since fallen into the sea and abandoned even by the Crusaders. They formed a natural swimming pool among the uneven rocks along the coast. Under the moonlight the sea was tamed, flecked here and there with the reflection of brightness.

'Look at the places where I take you,' said Ada. 'A handicraft factory for Yemeni women, a concert hall which was serving the purpose of a Viennese institute of psychotherapy, and now a Roman ruin under the moonlight. Jews have a gift for exile. Even their national home has this distinction, that you see things which are somehow still just beyond your reach, they have evaded you because they're really not quite yours, neither the Yemeni crafts nor the Viennese music. Not quite yours too, because you've wanted them so much.'

We walked on to a small mole which might have been pounded out by the tides of the centuries, or laid carefully by the Romans to shelter their galleys—it was impossible to distinguish in the dark. Ada was lifting aside her skirts as she stepped on to the jetty. For a moment we stood looking at the cowed sea. 'I couldn't feel anything but an exile here,' said Ada, 'even after everything that has happened to make me live here. I'll have misled you, I'm afraid, showing you things like this. But you'll see the superficial life easily enough, you hardly need people to show you tractors and that kind of thing. Probably it's not all superficial any more but quite essential, and I just take that sort of condition for granted.' Holding on to my arm in case she slipped, she turned round and began to walk back. Our footprints lay erratic in the sand, and uneven where Ada's heels had sunk in deeply. 'The truth is that I'd much rather live somewhere else, but there isn't anywhere else where I can live now. Don't misunderstand me, I wouldn't leave Israel or even want to go back to Vienna if someone gave me the opportunity, and because of this absolute certainty I won't take the German money they're always pressing on me. The slate can't be wiped clean, I can't go home, I can't live anywhere except here and I'm here only because the slate can't be wiped clean. So it goes on.'

'Lots of people make this their home,' I said.

'There are a lot of brave people, you need to be brave to be a successful exile.' We were silent, following our tracks along the soft line of the sea. 'I don't believe this, I feel it.' After stopping to admire the empty land and sky and sea, Ada grew more cheerful and made the excuse that the Viennese music had produced this effect on her. 'With the young here it's quite something different!' She was herself again. 'They're a decent, healthy, hardworking lot. Wonderful to see, especially for a nervous old woman like me. All you need to think is that you met a traveller from an antique land, two trunks of stone, headless in the desert, how does it go? You'll know a lot better than I will.'

The path seemed a steeper climb up than it had been descent and Ada wanted to take frequent rests. With the exertion, she loosened the fox fur and at the top, she sat down on a tuft of grass, telling me that I would have to fetch the car because she was too exhausted to take another step. The voices which we had heard earlier had followed us

along the top of the cliff and we fell in with two young men
and a girl playing hide-and-seek among the bunkers and the
heather. They had been swimming and their hair was all
dishevelled: one boy was still in his bathing costume with a
sweater thrown round his wet shoulders.

When I came back, carefully steering the car over the
bumpy ground, Ada was talking to the girl. 'She wants to
come with us to Tel Aviv, and I said that she could. Her
young men live here and they've already disappeared.'
Holding her wet towel in a bundle, the girl slipped gracefully
into the back of the car, the long damp hair clinging round
her neck. Before getting in, Ada swept a hand dramatically
round the open space, as much as to say, 'A blasted barracks,
a ruined mosque, and this pretty girl—take it or leave it.'
Then she elaborately brushed the sand off her dress and did
her best to clean the little button-boots. We drove off,
slowly making for the main road.

We said nothing on the way back, except for one last
remark of Ada's. She had been humming in a low voice an
old nursery tune:

> *Ach, du liebe Augustine,*
> *Augustine,*
> *Lieb' ist weg,*
> *Leb' ist weg,*
> *Augustine liegt im Dreck*
> *Ach, du liebe Augustine,*
> *du bist so schön.*

I told her that I had been brought up on this song, and
quickly she answered, 'Well, how would you translate it?
I'll work it out at my office tomorrow and let you have the
new version.'

The highway was deserted and we sped into Tel Aviv.
The only movement came from the huge blue neon sign of
the Delek petrol station, which stood high on the horizon,
winking into the night. I dropped the girl at the triumphal
Welcome arch, before turning off towards Ruppin Street.

Chapter Three

YOSSELE SCHUMACHER

THE FIRST NEWSREEL WHICH I saw in Israel showed the swept, austere flat of the Schumacher family; the anonymous but groomed figures of the parents, only slightly smudgy in the film, and their young daughter. On the wall was a photograph of their kidnapped son, Yossele, who would not, as the commentator said in the plummy tones reserved for newsreels, be spending *Pesach*, or the Passover, with his family. His whereabouts were still unknown. The audience hissed and shouted, although I later discovered that in this particular Haifa cinema it was the normal custom to express opinions throughout films.

The main film was *Exodus* and it was received with surprise as if those in the seats could hardly recognise these epic adventurers on the screen. It had been a routine trip for most of the immigrants crowding in, and the young men and women were by and large indifferent. But I was not prepared for Marcel, next to whom I was sitting. In the dark he loomed a bulky shape, finished off with a beret to complete the round silhouette. Through most of the first part, he was snoring. As the lights were turned on for the interval, I was confronted by this large unmistakable Frenchman, swelling out of his clothes, his fat face blurry with the unshaven stubble. It turned out that he came from Morocco. Almost immediately he opened his briefcase and began to sell me some charity tickets for his organization. I looked at the name; The Holy School of Rabbi Yokanaan, in the Holy City of Tiberias; and I saw that he was selling these tickets by authority of Our Righteous Teacher, the Rabbi from Stolin. Marcel took my note, creasing it into a crammed wallet, but he had no change and left the cinema hall to fetch some. The woman behind tapped me on the shoulder. 'You'll never see that again, he's a well-known confidence trickster.' She leant back smugly, but just before the lights dimmed, and I had given up hope, Marcel returned, edging his ungainly way into his seat. My change was sticky with the melting ice which he had swallowed on the way. 'You didn't expect to see me, did you?' he beamed.

All through the last part of *Exodus*, Marcel kept awake. He understood none of it, and obliged me to interpret for him. Some of Marcel's questions, thrown at me in a jovial, loud-toned French, were not easy to answer under cover of this vainglorious fantasy of a film. The United Nations vote puzzled him a good deal: what had these far-off countries got against Israel? And if the British had handed the affair over to the United Nations, why didn't they vote for the new state, if that was going to solve their problem? Marcel was not without intelligence, but his complete absence of historical knowledge was something pure. 'Hitler wasn't good for the Jews?' he asked at one point. 'What was getting into him? *qu'est-ce qu'il lui prenait?*' Marcel had left Morocco in 1953, and in spite of his appearance, he was now only twenty-three. His job was marvellous, he explained. The woman behind me was hardly able to contain herself during his long self-revealing speeches. Finally Marcel thought the film was *moche*, no good, and invited me to walk out and have a drink with him. I discussed this until the end of the film, when I promised to call on him at his flat one day. Not on the Sabbath, he asked, because he was religious.

The Schumacher case dragged on as it had already done for two years. Yossele was not home for the Passover; newspaper editorials were as censorious as ever; it was rumoured that the Israeli secret service had now been briefed to recover the boy from whatever hiding place he might be in. The most extraordinary aspect of the case, however, was the inflexible behaviour of Yossele's grandfather, Rab Nahman Shtarkes, already an old man of over seventy, and now held in prison on a charge of complicity in the kidnapping. Previously the old man had suffered at the hands of the Russians and the Germans, so that in a lifetime of persecution two years in a Jewish prison in Jerusalem was a short incident. It was his refusal to co-operate with the authorities, and his determination to have his own way over Yossele's religious education, which gave a certain stark grandeur to the kidnapping, the lying and the evasion. The grandfather declared in court that he was obeying the laws of God and was not concerned with the laws of man, a statement which stood out all the more poignantly because at the same time Eichmann was defending himself with the argument that he had been a follower of the laws of man, having no familiarity with the laws of God.

Rab Nahman Shtarkes lived in Mea Shearim, the orthodox religious quarter of Jerusalem. He was a firmly devout Jew, a member of the dwindling but fanatic community huddled into cramped streets and crowded courts, pressed among synagogues and religious schools—the *yeshivas* which provide their education of Bible reading and scholasticism—in surroundings virtually unchanged since Jerusalem was Turkish and pious Jews went there to study and live in sanctity and finally to be buried in the Holy Land. His children had all been given a traditional religious upbringing which fitted them for this confined and conventional piety. Only his daughter had failed to come up to his strict requirements by marrying Alter Schumacher, a poor Russian tailor whose religion, although orthodox, was more liberal. Yet when the Schumachers came to Israel in the early 1950s, they went to stay with the old man while looking for work and a house. Such family tensions as existed remained latent. It took Schumacher some time to find a job, and even longer to get settled. There was an acute housing shortage, and small prospects of relief. It was this period of confusion which later enabled Rab Nahman Shtarkes to accuse his son-in-law of intending to return to Russia. Meanwhile the old man was given the charge of Yossele and entrusted with his education as a result. Yossele was made to grow side-curls, to wear a skull-cap and breeches with cross-belts coming over his shoulders like any other small boy in Mea Shearim. At weekends his parents would visit him in Jerusalem, but did little else for the boy, hoping that soon they would have him under their own roof.

When his parents were firmly fixed in their new life, they sent for Yossele. By this time Alter Schumacher had found work and Mrs Schumacher was an assistant at a photographer's store. They had moved into a new apartment block in Holon, a suburb to the south of Tel Aviv, springing up along the sandy coast and rapidly expanding to take new immigrants. Yossele was put down for the Mizrachi school at Holon where he would receive a religious education, but one less determinedly orthodox than in Mea Shearim. It would not necessitate side-curls, for instance. The old man believed that the boy's soul would be endangered if he returned to his parents, and he took the necessary steps for his salvation, according to his lights. He arranged for the boy to disappear: Yossele was taken incognito by his uncle, Shalom Shtarkes, to a religious settlement and hidden there, only to vanish into thin air when the Schumachers insisted on having their son back. Mrs Schumacher had argued with her father for six months. She had waited in vain until, unable to continue this losing struggle with her adamant father, she had gone to the police. At first the police were reluctant to intervene in what appeared a family squabble, aggravated by factional religious differences—in the past the police have been too easily accused of discrimination against the orthodox. As the case became publicised, and opinion in the country aroused, Yossele became a national symbol for religious intolerance, and the police were left with no alternative but to take action. But by then it was too late, and all traces of the missing boy had been obscured. Rab Nahman Shtarkes was held in custody, for he made no secret of his connivance. He refused to answer questions in court, and the further charge of contempt of court left him indifferent. Contempt was exactly what he felt. Detained in prison, he saw no reason to alter his conduct, or to confess what he had arranged for the boy, while making it clear that he knew what had happened, and where Yossele was at present. His son Shalom had gone to London, and was arrested there on a kidnapping charge and held in Brixton pending the extradition order. It was assumed that Yossele had been secreted into the orthodox community at Stamford Hill, but again there was no evidence. Yossele was enshrouded in rumours.

Slowly a police case was built up. It was ascertained that Shalom Shtarkes had in fact taken Yossele from his grandfather's house in Jerusalem to Komemiut, a religious settlement in the country. A witness, called Kugeler, came forward to say that he had driven the boy and his uncle to Komemiut in his taxi. On the other hand, Kugeler was an unreliable and suspect witness who was turning informer in the sense that he was a renegade from this religious *moshav*. Nevertheless he claimed to have delivered the boy to Rabbi Mendelssohn, the religious leader of Komemiut, and that from the rabbi's house the boy had been escorted to the house of a ritual slaughterer for the community, a man called Kutt.

Proceedings were confused, although out of the allegations it seemed indisputable that Yossele had been to Komemiut, and as much came to be admitted in court. Rabbi Mendelssohn claimed that it was the traditional habit to take in strangers from other religious communities without asking questions, and of course, he had no idea who Yossele was. Moreover an uncle depositing his nephew in such a community was not an intrinsically suspicious event. In court, however, everybody prevaricated, going back on previous statements, giving fresh interpretations, or offering tiny new facts which altered the balance of several closely-connected stories, for they were all intimately concerned in the disappearance of the boy, of whom there was no trace, for he had gone to ground after leaving Komemiut. The detective-story excitement of the case was matched by the rising heat of public opinion. There was even an element of Jew-baiting as the orthodox were stopped in the street and insultingly asked to produce Yossele, and one outraged pious Jew took legal action after such an incident in public. Most of the vehemence of feeling derived from the political nature of the case. Ben Gurion's Mapai party has kept in power through its coalition with the National Religious Party, or Mizrachi. In return for this support, the government has made concessions to the religious which involve considerable restrictions on civil liberty. It is impossible to get a civil marriage in Israel, and an Israeli who wishes to marry someone who is not a Jew—however agnostic they may be themselves—will have to go abroad for a ceremony which will even so not be recognized in Israel. There is no public transport on the Sabbath; there is a Ministry for Religious Affairs; and a strict surveyance of kosher food, applying even to meals served on El Al aeroplanes. Hostility to the horse-trading between the Mapai party and the religious factions found its focus in the kidnapping of Yossele and the ineffective prosecution of the case.

At the time, while the case against Rabbi Mendelssohn and those involved with him was on, I met a journalist who had taken it upon himself to present Mrs Schumacher's story to a world which initially had not responded. At first many people held that she must carry the responsibility for leaving her son in the hands of the old man whose views on education and upbringing she knew all too well. Furthermore there was the unexplained delay in reporting the kidnapping to the police. Why had she not gone to them at once? This journalist was a neighbour of hers, and had persuaded her of the importance of full publicity. He had undertaken to make her plight notorious on the grounds

that even if she had committed mistakes, a two-year deprivation of her son was punishment enough. This was an almost
classic case of a journalist acting as a lever to general opinion.
A meeting was arranged for me with Mrs Schumacher.

Before going to see her, I went to call on the chief spokesman for the police. The Tel Aviv headquarters of the police
is in a large rambling block made up of right angles and long
corridors—a series of bunkers thrown together, reminiscent
of the English colonial authority which had constructed it.
Policemen stood guard around, looking squat and powerful
in their British-styled khaki uniforms and peaked forage
caps. They wore revolvers. I was shown up into an office
painted a heavy green, cluttered with desks and filing
cabinets. Another man shared this room with the police
spokesman, and beyond him the door swung wide to reveal
a busy collection of clerks and secretaries. Overhead a huge
fan rotated slowly, like an animal stranded on its back and
feebly waving its legs in the effort to right itself. The police
spokesman wore the rank of a colonel. He was sweating:
the fan made little difference to the temperature of the office.

Our conversation was in German, which he spoke with a
hard, correct accent. It began with a summary of the
incidents leading up to the civil court case between parents
and grandparents which ended in the High Court decision
that the old man must hand the boy back. The police were
in a very difficult position, he explained, for they could not
risk being labelled as the persecutors of the religious, but
it was quite untrue that they had deliberately dawdled in
the hope that the affair would drag itself to a standstill.
Mrs Schumacher herself was very difficult too; it was not as
simple as it looked, for she had her interests. When I asked
him if this was intended to mean that Mrs Schumacher was
dishonest, he nodded. It was not impossible then, in his
view, that there was some family conspiracy here? He
nodded again, but would not substantiate his innuendoes.
The police spokesman had a tiny twitch under his eye, as
if a small spring were operating the lid. It betrayed the smile

set across his features. Still, he went on, nobody could have expected the witness Kugeler, whose deposition was the only solid evidence concerning Yossele's movements, to turn out so unstable. Freely he had declared that he had been the chauffeur of the taxi driving Yossele to Komemiut. Only when interrogated in the High Court, Kugeler had recently taken back his evidence before the Attorney General. There was nothing left but to accuse him of perjury.

With the retraction of the only evidence, the police case fell to the ground. Shrugging his shoulders, the police spokesman explained that the fanatics had access to large sums of money, paid from London and New York. How else could they afford the expenses of the case? Witnesses were expensive too. Yossele might be anywhere now: he was certainly not in Israel, for they had combed the country. It was easy to fake a passport. Not that he himself had anything against religious orthodoxy, I must understand, he would never condone insult or violence to them, and he was proud of his descent from pious Jews. His grandfather had been a man like Rab Nahman Shtarkes. But Israel was a complex question of state-building, with an urgent time factor, so that all ends were justified in removing any obstacles. Law was the basis of the state and had to be demonstrated as such. The little tic flickered under his eye, a private Morse code of distress. The police, he admitted, had reached an impasse. If he could ever do anything for me. . . . Under the swishing fan, we shook hands, and I left the building, leaving my security pass with the guards.

II

Rabbi Mendelssohn was acquitted although the judge read him a lecture about civic duty. Considering that these inhabitants of Komemiut were the only people known to have seen the boy since his disappearance, it was an abstruse and rather academic exhortation. So it was with some trepidation that I went that week to keep the appointment with Mrs Schumacher. The affair appeared to have swirled back into its former evasiveness. I drove out of Tel Aviv down the long straight road to Holon, to the flat of the journalist who was to introduce us. It was in a brand-new three-storeyed house on the outskirts of the suburb with a view from the balcony over some flat dunes. The interior was cool and whitewashed, with modern furniture sparsely placed to give an impression of size. He had not returned from work, so that by the time I eventually reached Mrs Schumacher's after waiting for him, we were an hour and a half late, and the sticky, humid night had closed around us.

The Schumachers lived in a large apartment block some few hundred yards away, off a long and tree-shaded boulevard in the centre of the new town. Although modern, the concrete was already discoloured and the lines of the massy architecture were blurred under premature disintegration. The subdued orange lighting increased the melancholy of the little bare-rubbed path up to the side door, of the corridors and staircases with streaky walls, the interior courtyard scattered with odds-and-ends and the abandoned rubbish of a children's daytime playground. But Mrs Schumacher's flat was well cared for, if modest: it was recognizable from the remembered newsreel which had flickered on the screen some months before in Haifa. The photograph of Yossele still smiled cheerfully down from the wall, and an extra chair was somewhat consciously placed at an empty corner of the table. The sitting-room was rather cramped and we sat round in a close group while Mrs Schumacher told her story in Yiddish. She was a stocky, powerfully built woman, with a surprising quickness of manner, and an energetic voice which expressed her obvious strength. By comparison her husband was withdrawn and shy, although when he began to take up the conversation later in the evening he showed the tenacity of his convictions.

At that particular moment Mrs Schumacher's chief cause for distress was the recent acquittal of Rabbi Mendelssohn of Komemiut. There was no doubt in her mind that Yossele had been taken to the village and that the accused had arranged his subsequent disappearance as part of a carefully organized conspiracy. Vigorously certain that the affair was now political and had nothing to do with the return of her son, she believed that the police had bungled the case and claimed that they had done it on purpose. She had not liked to go to the police in the first instance because she had been unable to believe that her father would be capable of such an action. It was he who was responsible for the accusation that they had been intending to return to Russia because they preferred the conditions there—this was ridiculous, for if it were true, then why would they have spent years getting settled in Israel, finding jobs and a flat and inscribing Yossele for a religious school, when they could have lived with the old man and not cared about such things? She felt especially bitter with her father for raising this slander. Although she was an obedient daughter, there had always been friction over religious issues, and more so between her moderate husband and her intransigent father. This slander deprived her of any hope that the old man might relent, and this had sent her to the police. Mrs Schumacher's forceful appearance gave weight to her anger, and her face expressed her emotions clearly. Much less eloquently, her husband assented. With a wave of his hand, he declared that he had no time for all that religious nonsense, and any faith he might once have possessed had been pulled to shreds by this affair. Didn't we think that it was irreligious to separate parents and children? In the darkening room, lit by the bulbs of the wooden wall-brackets, we agreed.

The harsh Yiddish flow was broken by the arrival of their daughter from an evening ceremony at her school where she had been receiving a prize for Bible study. A quiet and dumpy fifteen-year-old girl stood awkwardly in the doorway, but only for a moment in order to lay her prize book on the nearby dresser and to announce that she was going out with her friends. Mrs Schumacher sighed that it was awful for the girl to listen to all the fuss being made over her brother. It depressed her and undermined her confidence. She felt unwanted so that now after two years she had come to resent Yossele. And once they had made an attempt to kidnap her. Somebody in the street just outside the house had asked her if she'd like to see her brother and wouldn't she like to go and play with him? A car was waiting but she had had the good sense to run away. They'd stop at nothing. Mrs Schumacher laid great emphasis on the organized conspiracy against her. Apparently one of the rabbis of the Agudat Yisrael, the orthodox religious party, a man who was also a member of the Knesset, and therefore an influential man in the country, had approached her with a bargain that they should keep Yossele and bring him up but she should have permission to visit him once a fortnight. Documents were prepared for signature, but she had been advised against this pact, on the grounds that they would not be likely to keep their word, but would use her signature to argue that she had abdicated her maternal rights. Yossele had been in Israel up till then, she was sure, and they had only panicked recently, sending him abroad. The government stood behind them, because otherwise their coalition would break; even if they weren't religious, all of them, they were all birds of the same feather, all politicians. Becoming very upset, Mrs Schumacher left the room to fetch some grapes and to prepare some coffee. Besides anything else, murmured the journalist to me, this affair had cost her a small fortune in entertaining people like us. Public subscriptions, however, paid for her legal costs.

When she returned, Mrs Schumacher retold the whole story, and was taken up by her husband who amplified it until we must have been over every detail a good many times. Mrs Schumacher was a woman slow to be aroused, and whose reactions might not crystallize for quite a long time, but once her mind was made up, there would be no relenting. Her conviction that a good many people knew where Yossele was, and were concealing it for their own ends, brought her pugnacity to the fore. More self-controlled but smouldering with anger and disappointment, her husband supported her. It was midnight before I left, by which time the injustice and impotence of her position had worked us all into an almost hysterical fatigue. Mrs Schumacher came downstairs insisting that then and there we should all drive off to her lawyer in case there was some aspect of the case which she or we had misrepresented. Standing on the pavement, she was still arguing excitably, and even got into the journalist's car to drive off to Tel Aviv. We pleaded the lateness of the hour. Anything to get Yossele back, she was saying, and imploring us to write as powerfully and as often as we could. Eventually her husband persuaded her that nothing could be gained from waking the lawyer up, and we stood quiet for a moment in the deserted street. A hundred yards away was a roundabout which joined the street to the main boulevard. The orange fluorescent lighting emphasized its contour, throwing a black circle of shadow. As we were saying good-bye, a low saloon car swung into the street. It was the police. They had arrived to announce that the Israeli security force had tracked Yossele down and had discovered him that very evening in the house of an orthodox Hassidic rabbi in Brooklyn. Yossele's identity still needed confirmation, but the boy was being held. We drove back into Tel Aviv and sat in a neon-lit *espresso* café off Dizengoff Square. It was so late that most of the chairs had been stacked on the tables, and a woman was mopping the floor. The journalist had missed an appointment by more than two hours. It could wait.

III

The next day I arranged to meet the lawyer who had successfully defended Rabbi Mendelssohn. At seven o'clock that evening I was waiting in the sleek bar of the Sheraton Hotel, secreted in its air-conditioned and glass-walled luminosity. All day rumours about Yossele had been circulating. It was speculated that he would be exchanged by the American authorities for Dr Robert Soblen, the unfortunate spy who had sought refuge in Israel under the Law of the Return which permits all Jews to claim Israeli nationality: or that although Yossele had now been unearthed, he would not be allowed to leave New York because he had been smuggled in. There were the first reports of his kidnapping from Komemiut. Apparently he had been disguised as a girl in the settlement, his side-curls were combed out and he was put into a dress. Then he had been entrusted to a French-woman, a Christian who had become converted to Hassidism and had gone to live in Mea Shearim. A photograph of Yossele had been stuck into her passport and she had flown with him to New York; a mother and daughter paying respects to orthodox cousins in the guise of this rabbi and his family of seven children. Yossele had been there in anonymity ever since. Throughout the day I had discussed the news, and now sat in the oddly empty hotel with an Arab friend whom I had run into, wondering why the guests seemed to glide as insubstantial as ghosts.

There was nothing insubstantial about the lawyer when he arrived. A thick-set, muscular man, he was not exactly turning to fat, but presented a complacent, unused frame. Behind the clean-cut chin hesitated the roll of a second, like a drop of water coagulating before falling. He was very smartly dressed, in clothes probably from America or England, which added to the effect of self-presentation, as if he were anxious to give a fluent portrait of himself. The only facts which I had discovered about him were that he was a former member of the terrorist Irgun organization, and that when he was about twenty, he had been captured and interned in Kenya for three years.

On sitting down, he ordered a bowl of nuts, and before speaking, he would push a handful or two into his mouth, and then ruminate, with occasional words coming indistinctly through his munching. It gave him time to weigh up what he was saying. At the outset he explained that he was not in any way religious, but rather an agnostic, although he could respect strong convictions when he saw them, and these orthodox Jews fascinated him. Furthermore there was a case to be made out for them, and it was a political one, which was what had attracted him. As he saw it, Ben Gurion was becoming a dictator; he laid great emphasis on this, asserting that the prime minister had been unfit for his office for a good many years, now that he attributed to himself messianic powers which he clung to with the determination of the senile—the nearest analogy was Adenauer. The liberty of the subject in Israel was at stake, even the survival of democratic government. The Agudat Yisrael party might consist of fanatics, cranks if you will, but even fanatics had a right to be heard. The government had used the old device of stirring up a diversion to detract from a main issue—exciting unpopularity against the religious in order to conceal the establishment of one-man, one-party rule. The Yossele case made excellent political capital for Ben Gurion, he maintained, and for this reason he had decided to defend the accused. It was a great chance for the judicature to exercise its traditional function as a check to the executive, or in other words, to bring down the government.

To his satisfaction, he had destroyed the police case, and exposed their flimsy pretences. The only evidence which the police had produced in court had been retracted. He made it clear to me that he believed Kugeler had been subjected to some illegal methods in order to extort this statement in the first place. Through the heavy chewing of nuts and with much insinuation, he hinted at abominable ties between government and police: he never doubted the official use of third degree. First the government had prevaricated in order to stay in power by maintaining the coalition, and then it had sought to subdue the extremists once and for all by rigging the case. It was perfectly clear to him and he had been glad to stand in Ben Gurion's way.

Things were not all quite as straightforward as they seemed in the Schumacher family, he could agree with the colonel of police to that extent. Behind the scenes were motives so entangled that he could hardly clarify them, although it was virtually certain, for instance, that the Schumachers intended returning to Russia. Unfortunately he could not reveal his sources of information, for these were behind the Iron Curtain, and the safety of some agents might be prejudiced. Of course there was an extensive unofficial communication, the Russians were always helpful, he said, eyeing me to see what effect this might have—they were sensitive about anything Jewish. Then again, he had recently made a trip to New York, where the existence of Yossele had been known for a long time, as he discovered, but the authorities were holding on to him for some private reasons. Secret service agents had tracked him down with no trouble, so the delay must have originated in a cabinet decision. To him, Mrs Schumacher was by no means as silly and hysterical as she appeared to his colleagues. Perhaps she was quite happy to be rid of the boy and all the expenses of bringing him up, perhaps the whole affair had been rigged and she had been in league with her enemies. I told him that such suppositions were fantastic—after an evening spent with her, they were merely slanderous. With a great handful of nuts, he deliberated. Did I know of the secret meetings between Mrs Schumacher and the Agudat Yisrael representatives? He knew all the people involved, and all the proposals, and if she had been serious in her intention to recover the boy, Mrs Schumacher would never have negotiated in this way. The acquittal of Rabbi Mendelssohn was really the last stage in these negotiations. If the rabbi had not been acquitted, Yossele would not have returned: in a way it was almost embarrassing that the events were separated by only two days. Still—he laid his finger across his nose and grinned—the tissue of lies and accusations and contradictions could not be resolved or substantiated, because there were too many powerful interests now involved. After two years, all he knew for hard fact was the method of behaviour of the present government. If it were true, I asked him, that the government wished to exploit this situation for its own ends, why hadn't the religious leaders, so clever on other political occasions, been able to prevent it? But the clock struck: it was time to stop. The lawyer took me by the arm to the main hall of the Sheraton, where I saw the reason for the hotel's unusual emptiness. The rooms had been reserved for scores of orthodox Jews, all men, who were now assembling. They were to have a celebration dinner in honour of their victory in court, and the rabbi and his fellow-accused were among the prominent guests. In their black clothes, with heavy square-cut overcoats in spite of the heat, all with wide hats, they came trooping into the hotel, excitedly talking. Pushing our way through the crowd, we looked for the rabbi, and I was in time to see a thin figure with a black beard and pointed cheek-bones disappearing into the dining-room. I would have to meet him another time: the lawyer shrugged his apologies, and excused himself—the meal was due to begin and he had to take his place at the table of honour punctually, for as a non-religious man he did not wish to give cause for any offence. I said that I was glad to notice how lavish the preparations were, that religious enthusiasms did not encourage abstin-ence, nor the misapplication of funds. He smiled and, opening his hand, dropped the last remaining nuts on to the expensive felt carpeting. I went to find my Arab friend who had been waiting in the lounge, and we left.

Outside more guests were getting out of taxis. It was July and the humidity was extreme. They mopped their faces, half-concealed under beard and hat, then turned through the glass doors into the air-conditioned comfort. About one hundred and fifty schoolchildren were demonstrating at the hotel entrance, marching up and down to taunt the guests with cries and placards: 'Yossele, welcome home.' No adults joined in, except for a schoolteacher or two, and the demonstration was fairly orderly. Apparently the children had thrown stones to begin with, but they had been res-trained. In their thick overcoats, though, the late arrivals broke into a run, either from fear of the children, or anxiety that they would miss the feast laid out in the hotel which gleamed out its expensive modern glossiness into the surrounding night.

'I am sure you didn't find out anything,' said my Arab friend, as we drove off.

'Nothing I could rely on,' I said, 'I see why they were acquitted in court though.'

'I could have told you that before you started,' he said. We went to have dinner, sitting in the open air, but it was too stifling to argue, for all facts, opinions, prejudices, to say nothing of logic with which to marshal them, seemed to have melted into a uniform haze, into the shimmering aspects of a long Oriental tale which passed from mouth to mouth, embellished, diverting and amoral.

IV

Not long after I happened to be staying in the village of Nehora, and my eye accidentally falling on a regional map, I noticed that I was living only a few miles away from the religious *moshav* of Komemiut. Both Nehora and Komemuit are settlements in what has come to be known as the Lachish area, a wide expanse of land from the Gaza strip to the Israeli frontier below Jerusalem. It is the bottleneck of the country, a collar dividing the trunk stretching into the desert at the south and the elongated head and shoulders of the fertile north. At the centre of the Lachish area is the Faluja crossroads, controlling the approaches to Tel Aviv, to Jerusalem and to Beersheba. At this point—as a roadside notice proclaims—an Egyptian brigade was encircled in 1948 and forced to surrender. One of its officers was Major Nasser. Since that date, an interlocking of settlements has been devised to colonize the area and to offer protection against the constant infiltration of *fedayeen* from Gaza or from Jordan. For a good many years, this was the recognized route for smugglers and trouble-makers, so that people were reluctant to settle here, and roads were unsafe at night. The land, however, is rich, and with proper irrigation can be reclaimed, so that there is a double incentive to colonize it.

There is nothing homogenous about these settlements: they are on the contrary more of an experiment in social cohesion, for new immigrants from dozens of countries have been put down here. Some of the villages are Czech or Persian by nature, others are inhabited by former cave-dwellers from the island of Djerba or by Cochin Jews, while a few contain mixed populations. Hardly any of this wide range of people were former agricultural workers, and the Lachish area has therefore come to show, in its more intense manifestations, the problems of adaptation and social reorientation facing new immigrants in all aspects of their lives, sex and marriage customs, language, work, the manners of daily existence. Going from village to village it is usual to hear stories about the behaviour of the neighbours—how they put their prayer shawls into the sacred refrigerators, or all rushed to the bank in a communal panic that they had been defrauded by opening accounts.

Komemiut is one of some dozens of these villages, carefully located to be a few miles equidistant from a service town, and the service towns in their turn rely on Kiryat Gat, the capital of the Lachish area and the focus of its initial industry. Having already spent some time in the area visiting other settlements I drove to Komemiut one Friday. At the turning off the main road stood an elderly woman and a girl, asking for a lift which I gave them. The track down to Komemiut began with asphalt, turned into packed and sun-dried earth and ended as a rutted and pitted direction. On either side the fields were broad and unhedged, rolling away into the distance. Stubble paled the colours down to a uniform ochre which presented the only alternative to the beady blue of the sky. The wheat harvest was already in: the stubble would turn to the sticky brown of treacle under the fierce sun. In the simplicity of this landscape, so flat and regular and two-toned, the multiple complexity of Israeli fields and agriculture—smallholdings and strips with varied crops all crammed together—seemed to fall away. The countryside changed: the present was transformed. Instead Komemiut

seemed the reincarnation of the *shtetl*; it was a transplanta-
tion or a reconstruction of the typical little village in the
Pale where the Jews had been segregated on the fringes of
Russia. This was almost the only corner of the country where
such an illusion was possible. This featureless monotony
belonged to Central Europe; the little cluster of ragged
houses scattered around the end of the bumpy track had an
affinity not with Israel but with Galicia. The Pripet marshes
should have been over the skyline. Komemiut was the
novels of Sholem Aleichem come to life.

At the farthest point of the village I dropped the girl and
the elderly woman. They disappeared into one of the huts:
from behind the curtains I could see faces peeping at the
strangers in his car. I felt like a Russian official intruding
into the cloistered world of the community. But by the time
that I had turned my car round at the place where the track
gave out into the open fields, the girl had come running back
excitedly. She wanted to know if I would like her to guide
me round Komemiut, for it seemed a pity to have come so
far in my taxi and not to see the sights. I tried to explain that
my car was not a taxi, but she was unwilling to believe me.
How was it possible that a car should not be a taxi?

The girl was fifteen. She was extremely pretty, in a delicate
rather chiselled way. The bones of her face were prominent,
and emphasized by her thinness. She was fair with dark
lustrous eyes which shone with her vivacity and were the
most obvious expression of her gay temperament. Short,
cropped hair bounced on top of her head with her quick
movements. That day she had been shopping with her aunt
in Tel Aviv, she explained, but she was glad to get back
home because she didn't like big towns. They only went up
there rarely, although she'd also been to Jerusalem, which
was wonderful. Buses were unpleasant but she had been very
glad when I had stopped to give her a lift because they had
just got off the bus and would have had to walk the last
miles as taxis hardly ever came down the track. She was
wearing a grey woollen blouse which buttoned primly up to

her neck and down to her slender white wrists. Her heavy skirt reached well below her knees and black stockings concealed her legs. These were her everyday clothes, she told me, slightly surprised at the question. There was a Puritan cleanness and severity about them which contrasted poignantly with her liveliness.

As we drove slowly back through the rag-taggle outskirts of the village, she asked me to stop, and getting out of the car, she rushed into a house, to emerge with a giggling girl friend. Once they were together in the car—a two-door Morris minor—they showed off like carnival queens, waving out of the windows and making mock bows. Behind the lace curtains of the huts bobbed the disapproving faces of mothers. Very soon a crowd of small children was running behind the car, or holding on to it, catching at anything they could. Animals or chickens which had strayed on to the road were frightened off to the barns.

We spoke in Yiddish and I am not sure if the girls spoke Hebrew: with the aunt she had also spoken Yiddish. At a cowshed a young man in army uniform was cleaning out the stalls. He was wearing side-curls which dangled below his beret. The girl explained that any conscripts for national service were allowed to stay at Komemiut although they were enrolled into a kind of community unit because too many religious scruples prevented them from joining the ordinary army. In the distance I saw another soldier, red-faced and gigantic, riding a bicycle and giving a small child a lift on the handlebars. The girl was an informed source of gossip, for nothing in the community seemed to have missed her, and she pointed out all the huts and told me which family lived where, and what they did. The ritual slaughterer was walking towards us, she said, indicating a man with a full red beard; he was very important, his name was Kutt. Except for the soldiers, everybody was dressed as they would have been in the Hassidic world of two hundred years ago. Even the smallest boys chasing the car wore skull-caps, and there were no bare knees except mine. There was an intelligence and an alertness in Komemiut—not only in the searching eyes of the girl—which belied the dirty and ramshackle farmyard, the little random houses and the spacious desolation of the harvested fields. The village elders, coming to their front doors or meeting in conclave in front of the synagogue, ignored the car and its mob of chasing children. Mothers with long skirts, and rolled-down sleeves and kerchiefs, frowned but did not call them home.

Education obviously held a central place in daily life. Not only were the children required to satisfy the ordinary demands of the state education, but they also had to undergo the religious upbringing of the community. The girl showed us the religious school which all boys were compelled to attend. It stood at a short but commanding distance from the middle of the village, and was certainly its most imposing building. From its size, I had mistaken it for the granary. Next to the synagogue, on an open green whose grass had been trodden away, was Rabbi Mendelssohn's house, by far the most conspicuous private house in the village and second only to the school. The symmetrical windows in its neat brick facade were adorned with painted shutters, giving it an almost colonial-style appearance. I said to the girl that it was more than twice the size of any other house in Komemiut and she replied that this was true and also quite right and proper because Rabbi Mendelssohn was more than twice as wise as anybody else in the place. Sholem Aleichem would have been proud of her.

We drove to the bakery which she insisted that we should visit. Komemiut bakes the bread for Kiryat Gat and the surrounding countryside, thus ensuring that there are no kosher problems. Half a dozen men were at work in white aprons and white vests which left their arms bare, but they were all orthodox members of the village. Business was best at Passover, said the manager of the bakery, for then they exported their unleavened bread, *matzos*, to orthodox communities around the world; guaranteed kosher. It was growing late in the afternoon and I was nervous of staying in the village for the Sabbath would begin at sundown and then I would not be allowed to drive the car. The manager of the bakery began a long story about the difficulties of travelling, of getting past the customs. He had been to New York and to London recently, but it was difficult for him with his religious obligations and there was no place like home. Behind him, in the sinking light, men were rolling dough at a bench and then plaiting loaves. We went outside. 'Would you like to see where Yossele stayed?' asked the girl, her eyes bright with the remembered excitement. Her friend began to giggle once more, and the two of them gutturally discussed, in what they thought was an undertone, whether it was suitable to tell me the story. When she made up her mind after this short hesitation there was nothing self-conscious in her manner: perhaps she had no idea of the stir which had spread concentrically from the incident, once Yossele had dropped like a stone into the undisturbed waters of this village. Yes, they had all known when a strange little boy had arrived one night, the rabbi had spoken to them about it, but it hadn't seemed odd, just interesting. He'd been put to sleep in the Kutts' house, she pointed out the anonymous building among a lot of other one-floor whitewashed cubes, with an ungainly verandah along the roadside. Yossele was very nice when she'd met him, but he'd spent a lot of time with the rabbi and the others and she hadn't seen much of him—he had disappeared very quickly too. In the synagogue she'd seen him; he looked like any-body else, that was all she could say. They had all been asked not to talk about him, she added.

As if anxious to continue pointing out village landmarks, to make Komemiut seem more interesting, she went on: 'Do you see those houses over there?' pointing at two bungalows not far away on the other side of the path. '*Dort woihnen die Goyim.*' I asked her who these *Goyim*, or Gentiles, might be, so carefully housed just outside the confines of the village. She explained that they were the people hired to do the work that the Scriptures forbade the pious to perform.

71

Principally it was work on the Sabbath, when they had to milk the cows and run the farm—she smiled enchantingly, as if it were the most normal thing in the world. And then told me that of course if one couldn't work because the Bible said so, then one had to hire somebody. Who were these people to be hired, these Gentiles? Oh, Israelis, she answered in a matter-of-fact voice, as if the question were superfluous. I hadn't the heart to ask what she thought she was: to her still uncomplicated mind such a situation posed no problems.

When I dropped the girls back at their homes, their mothers were waiting, furious and peremptory. The girls hardly had time to get out of the car before they were dragged off. No children were now playing in the farmyard or running after the car. In the late afternoon the sun was slanting over the bare fields. My friend waved from the doorway: she was certainly in for trouble. The men were congregating outside the synagogue as I drove past—black upright figures who stared at the car. At the far end of the village, as I bumped my way along the track, I was again stopped by someone asking for a lift, this time a young man elegant in tight trousers and a clean white shirt. He turned out to be one of the men kept for work which offended against the religious conscience. Although it was Friday evening and the Sabbath was therefore beginning, he was going in to Kiryat Gat. I asked him what it was like to work at Komemiut but he was taciturn, as much as to say that one job was much the same as another, and I left him at the Faluja crossroads, a slim young man under the sign proclaiming the Egyptian surrender.

Back at Nehora, only a few miles across the fields, it was considered something of a feat of daring to have braved the village of Komemiut, since very few local people went there in the face of the hostility of the inhabitants. If I had stayed there after sunset, I was told, I would certainly have run into trouble when I had driven my car out, perhaps I would have had stones thrown at me, or even worse. Foolhardiness could go no further: there was no reasoning with the fanatics; and I was asked if I had heard the latest scandal about them. They who were so strict in all their religious observances and were so horrified by the idea of pig-raising or pork-eating had been caught selling the waste from their bakery to a neighbouring kibbutz for pig-food. To maintain the fiction, though, the kibbutz claimed to be raising bears— religious logic is a law unto itself. There was trouble over the bakery too, it had been condemned, they refused to close it down, the authorities had intervened, there were rumours, scandal—to hear Nehora talk about Komemiut, it would have been possible to assume that it was a remote corner of another continent, still a part of the mythical Yiddish life of Central Europe which has now vanished.

V

By chance I saw the police spokesman once more towards the end of that summer. An Israeli friend of mine had suggested that I do some work on a documentary film, translating a French text into English. After lunching in Tel Aviv, I went out to the Herzlia Film Studios which were in the garden suburb, spreading the pretty net of villas and shrubs and domestication around the city. When I arrived, the producer and his cameraman and one or two others were already sitting in a small room with a screen installed. Then it took some time to locate the can of film, but just as we were due to start and the lights had already been switched off the door opened and in came the chief spokesman for the police in his colonel's uniform, accompanied by another colonel of police and a civilian. With many apologies, we were all cleared out, it was a matter of urgency, they explained to us, for they had to see a short film—only ten minutes if we would excuse them. The door locked us into the passage outside. Immediately we all went round to the projection room, where the new film was being wound on to the spool. It proved to be a newsreel, and it did indeed only last a short number of minutes. But it showed a violent and brutal sequence of people being forcibly ejected from their houses by the police. Peering down from the projection room, we saw scenes in this slum—possibly on the outskirts of Tel Aviv—with women gripping on to the doorposts and shouting defiance at the police. Some of the women were carried off bodily but one was dragged by her feet down a flight of steps, and in the process her clothes were torn up over her head. She appeared unconscious at the end of the ordeal but the film was too jerky to be certain. It had been shot with some difficulty, and the police seemed unaware of being filmed, for their truncheons were out and they were hitting round about when this short newsreel came to an end. Downstairs I came face to face with the police spokesman who made a show of surprised pleasure at seeing me, apologized for the inconvenience of turning us out of the studio, but 'had some routine work to get through.' The little spring in his eyelid was catching up and down, winking its distress signals. The colonel led him away: the censorship committee had to communicate its decision.

As I was writing this, the same Israeli friend who had suggested the translation of this script and who was therefore indirectly responsible for my witnessing this incident of government in the raw, sent me a press cutting with the High Court decision that this particular newsreel had been unjustly censored, and that it was in the public interest to project it.

I also saw Marcel once more, when I went to call on him at his flat in Nazareth. He lived in the new housing centre on the hill above the old Arab town, an Israeli outpost of rearing concrete blocks and clumps dominating the scene as if to control the unruly inhabitants of Nazareth. I explained to Marcel that I had sat next to him some months before at the film of *Exodus*, but he had already remembered, and began to spout back at me some of the explanations which I had given him at the time. His flat was two and a half rooms, that is to say that the entry formed a space in which to put a table—thereby accounting for the extra half. The flat was not very clean, and there was a smell of stale laundry. Marcel was married, he told me, but his wife was away. Once again I found it hard to believe that this bulbous and bloated man was only twenty-three. I interrupted his reminisences of *Exodus* to ask him again, but I had remembered correctly. 'Where's South Africa?' he asked suddenly. 'At the bottom of Africa,' I told him. 'And Africa?' 'Africa is where you once lived.' 'If it's part of Africa, I don't see the distinction between *Afrique* and *Afrique du Sud*?'

In the end I asked him what he thought of the Yossele Schumacher case. He scratched under his beret. '*Jamais entendu parler.*' Like most fat men, he had a nice smile. I told him about Yossele but he was not interested. Would I like to buy a ticket for the Holy school of Rabbi Yokanaan, in the Holy City of Tiberias, he asked me, for he was licensed to sell them by authority of Our Righteous Teacher the Rabbi from Stolin? I reminded him that I had already more than fulfilled any obligation I might have towards Rabbi Yokanaan's religious works.

'You think this is a bad job. You don't like me for it?' Marcel looked puzzled. To clear the expression off his face, I bought another ticket. Almost ignoring my note as he tucked it away into the thick wallet, he went on, 'But I like it, and I'm very good for the religious, *je suis très bon pour les religieux.*'

Rab Nahman Shtarkes was out of prison now, and Yossele was back with his parents, and going to school every day, one of the crowd. His public statement, made on the tarmac at Idlewild Airport to a mob of pressmen, was simple: '*Ich will ein guter Yid sein.* I want to be a good Jew.'

'*Très bien,*' said Marcel, when I told him. '*Très bien.*'

75

Chapter Four

EILAT

I

KING SOLOMON'S CAFÉ HOLDS the crossroads at Eilat, a kind of unofficial toll-gate, dominating the long, lonely approach to the town and cutting off the corner of the main road which forks towards the civic centre. Anybody who had been dropped after a lift through the Negev down from Beersheba or from the few outposts in the intervening desert goes in to the café: anybody hoping for a lift northwards settles down there to waste away the hot hours with Tempo lemonade, which stays cool as long as it takes to drink down at a reasonable speed. It is a hitch-hikers' paradise of corrugated iron, patched-up boardings, scrubbed wooden tables and benches, flies and a radio. There is nothing of the air-cooled sophistication to be found in the Arkia airlines' office at the hub of the civic centre, which functions like a local newspaper, disseminating information and gossip. Drinks served there stay cool as long as need be: it is an oasis where the inhabitants congregate. Talk at the King Solomon's, on the other hand, is slow and impersonal. The brain is sluggish under the tin roof: the eye is on the road except once an hour or so, when it turns to watch the aeroplanes drop out of the sky and swoop down on to the airstrip running along the valley.

At night there is very little traffic, unless it is a military convoy, because there is no protection against infiltrators and every now and again there is an incident; a truck is ambushed, a driver killed. After dark, King Solomon's café is isolated, abandoned on the outskirts. Only a few soldiers or merchant seamen sit outside—the lights are brighter elsewhere. The owner came from Morocco and keeps his wireless implacably fixed to Arab music, its jangling plainsong insistent in the night. It is too hot in that climate to want more than a sandwich to eat, and the town is small enough for acquaintances to offer the cups of coffee which take the place of a meal. The beach has a rival café with the added prospect of a slight breeze off the waves, and the smooth seawater is cold. Bathing at night brings gooseflesh, so unexpected that the body seems to have forgotten the motion and shudders as if to recapture the memory.

In Eilat I was staying in a room attached to a private house. It might have been a garage, for it did not communicate even though it was structurally incorporated into the low bungalow. The garden path ran up to its door, and then branched round to the entrance of the house, half-hidden by some scrawny shrubs, withering in the climate. Oblong and low, the room was suffocatingly hot when I first moved in. The cotton curtains sagged across the sides of the windows but could not be pulled further and so were no help in keeping the sun out. I lay naked on the grey blankets of the truckle-bed, fatigued by the slow rise and fall of my chest, its contours picked out with sweat. Behind a partition, there was a stand-up shower but the water would come out tepid by the time that the sun had boiled it up in the pipes. During the afternoon the supply was cut off at the mains, and all the time the water was red with rust, particularly out of the shower whose tap had almost eroded. Only in an emergency of thirst did I drink this strong and oxidic concoction, but the alternative was to walk down three blocks of new housing estate to the King Solomon for my food and drink. The best feature of the room—and the reason why I had taken it—was the electric air-cooler, square and chromium-functional, next to the bed. These coolers, which operate by water pumped through them, are now virtually a standard fixture in every house and flat in Eilat where they were introduced three or four years ago. Summers without such water-coolers—for the six or seven years at the beginning—were so intolerable that the original inhabitants can hardly remember how they put up with the hardship. Once too the water supply was suspended for four days in a blazing August. Seawater and Tempo were left to take care of all needs. But water-coolers are always temperamental and mine worked when it thought fit, until the owner of the house replaced it. He was one of the original founders of Eilat, an old-timer of thirty-four in a town where except for the mayor and harbourmaster there are no old. After ten summers, though, he knew the value of an efficient cooler.

At the time I was reading *The Letters of Oscar Wilde* which had just been published and which I was to review. Taking this thick volume and a shiny black notebook, slippery with the sweat of my palms, I would go down to the King Solomon after sunset to read in its shanty enclosure. The telegrams to Whistler, the polite little notes to Curzon or Millais, the period homilies: 'Make some sacrifice for your art, and you will be repaid; but ask of Art to sacrifice herself for you, and a bitter disappointment may come to you'— all blended with the Arab music to produce an improbable background. Wilde would have found this tinny and lopsided Israeli café very foreign and antipathetic. It was during one of these sessions, while I was copying sentences into the notebook, that I met Avner. He must have been watching me for some time beforehand, for the expression on his face was that of a man trying to understand behaviour which he approves although it looks absurd. In fact I never explained to his satisfaction why I was making notes out of an eight-hundred-page book. For him, the book was too large, the notes too small. Not that Avner was stupid or badly educated, although he admitted that he hadn't read anything except newspapers since he left school. His English was quite proficient. It was just that he disliked waste.

Avner's whole body quivered with controlled energy—
his uniform with its split seams and frayed edges made him
look as if he were on active service. Blue eyes were dug in
behind ridges in a handsome face, and his beard seemed all
the stronger because it was unexpectedly trim. Two bars on
his shoulder proclaimed that he was a lieutenant, but his
vitality and simplicity belonged more properly to a cadet.
Perhaps he had been chosen for his job because there was a
good deal of the boy scout in him. Once when I suggested
to him that all leaders had something retarded about them
or they wouldn't want to be leaders, he told me that he had
adopted the *Führerprinzip* as his own. He was prone to laugh
easily though, showing off very white teeth suddenly rising
behind his dark beard, but it was an athletic laugh, co-
ordinating a lot of muscles so that there was nothing jerky.
It was obvious that he was a good and professional soldier.
In fact he was an instructor at Beer Ora, a Gadna camp some
few miles along the road to the north. There was also a
military depot at Eilat and he used to drive between the two
places in a jeep which he had appropriated for himself,
stopping only at King Solomon's café. I never saw him pay,
and later came to suspect that the owner had his reasons
for giving him drinks.

Eilat was his natural habitat. The ferocity of the place
matched his high spirits, and this continuous tension kept
him happy. He had spoken to me in the first place only in
some spirit of challenge. Like an animal he was preoccupied
with immediate things. Consequences were no concern of
his so long as he was engaged in activity—soldiering, eating,
driving his jeep, talking, showing off. If he had been compelled to live elsewhere, and in another profession, he would
probably have come to a sticky end because of his contempt
of right-minded behaviour. In Eilat—hanging with difficulty on to the coast where Israel has this brief aperture into
the Red Sea—his gifts found an outlet in the rough, frontier
atmosphere. The copper-mines at Timna add to the adven-
turous spirit of the place, reminiscent of the elemental

virtues and vices of a nineteenth-century gold-rush town. 'And those who quit their proper sphere change their surroundings merely, not their natures. They do not acquire the thoughts or passions appropriate to the sphere they enter. It is not in their power to do so. Emotional forces are as limited in extent and duration as the forces of physical energy.' There was nothing in Oscar Wilde's *De Profundis* for a twenty-four year old *sabra* lieutenant.

Avner's friends were much like himself. Bronzed young men with vaulted ribs above thin hips, they got up at five in the morning, stopped work at eleven, swam for the rest of the day and talked into the night. Work cannot be performed systematically at Eilat, and besides, the people who live there are not those who fit into systems. From the first meeting in the café, I was taken on to be shown his friends. Still holding my books, I climbed the stairs of a three-storeyed apartment block. The young man who owned the flat was a face-worker in the Timna copper-mines. His fat-legged and dumpy girl friend was making coffee when we came in. Three or four others sat around on the floor. I joined them because the furniture looked unexpectedly spindly—too modern to use. Black-and-white Japanese prints were hung round the room: a collection of hothouse plants lined the windowsill. Nobody asked questions while we drank the coffee—to be with Avner was a passport to acceptance, although they inspected me politely to see what he had hooked this time.

It had been arranged that they were all to see a hypnotist who was giving a show that evening. The dumpy girl switched off the water-cooler and in the silence after its permanent hum, the heat began to filter through the flat, catching up with the steam of the coffee cups. We got up to leave and clattered down the concrete stairs on to the dusty road which still retained the heat of the sun's onslaught. In the little garden plots, plants and shrubs languished in hard black circles of earth as the water-sprinklers were turned on to the caked surfaces. At night, though, most of the immediate hardness disappears and the town looks almost pretty. The haphazard direction of the streets and the random placing of the houses, with no regard to the lie of the land, no longer looks forlorn but rather like an old city now being pulled together. We walked across to the open space in the centre, and on down towards the sea, to the open-air amphitheatre which has been built on a rise behind the harbour.

Under the black sky as thick as felt, almost the whole of Eilat had assembled to watch the hypnotist. The amphitheatre was a noisy and mobile swarm. The hypnotist, furthermore, knew hardly more Hebrew than the order to 'shut up!' and so operated through an interpreter, barking his orders out in English with a strong Glasgow rasp, and having them transmitted in a polite and soft-spoken Hebrew. At the call for volunteers at the start of the programme, Avner was at once up on the platform. There was a long and rowdy delay while various subjects were chosen out of the audience, during which Avner was calling up several of his friends. A squad of soldiers gathered, holding up their clasped hands in the approved way. When they were all eventually thrown off the stage, Avner still remained, to be laid on his back and trodden on in the pit of his stomach by the hypnotist. Reluctantly he came back to his seat, but with eyes bright with mischief. Having selected his victims, the hypnotist made them scratch, dance and play children's games, or stuck pins into them with no effect. But by then Avner was bored and had clambered round to the back of the amphitheatre to talk to more friends until inevitably he became involved in a quarrel with the hypnotist, which ended with the hypnotist climbing down into the audience to fetch Avner on to the stage where he tried once more to put him to sleep, while the soldiers roared their approval.

To celebrate his success, Avner insisted on taking the little group of his friends to the night club. No sooner was he in 'The End of the World', though, than he fell in with another friend, a former sailor who had lost an eye, and was therefore nicknamed Nelson. It seemed that Nelson had

decided to sail through the Suez Canal just because Nasser
had placed a ban on Israeli shipping. Joining a Danish
cargo-boat, he had made no secret of his intentions. As the
boat steamed through the canal, he had climbed the mast
with a camera and had photographed Port Said to prove
that he had completed his self-appointed mission. With
great forbearance, the Egyptian authorities arrested him and
imprisoned him for a few months. Avner told this story in
front of Nelson who received it as a statement of credentials.
The adventure was worth a lifetime of credit in an Eilat bar.
A busload of tourists jammed down the stairs into the
sticky cellar to listen to a singer. Candles drooped in the heat
into the form of croquet hoops, the molten wax running
over the tables. Folk-songs in Hebrew, French, Spanish and
American drummed around the underground cellar as the
tourists joined in. Avner, Nelson and the group had disappeared and so I slipped out, pushing up the staircase with
its *collage* designs and its scrawled lipstick signatures:
'Robert Graves was here.' 'So was Yigal.'

The streets were empty as I walked back. I had left the
water-cooler on in my room and its cold air was as sharp
as a disinfectant. I took a shower in the tiny concrete bunker,
but in the small space I knocked the lavatory seat as I did
so. It was loose, for the wooden ring had never been fixed
with hinges, and from underneath flew out an insect with
a five- or six-inch wingspan, half cockroach, half beetle,
whose antennae were almost twice as long as itself. It flew
with a singing note, like a piano tuner, and by the time I had
chased it, cornered it and flicked it to death with my towel,
the room was soaked and the night was well on into the
small hours. Nor would the lavatory flush this armoured
insect away, but it lay reproachfully intact in the few shallow
centimetres of rusty water at the bottom of the bowl for as
long as I lived in the room. Sometimes at crucial moments
it seemed to come alive again, for the plumbing had some
internal mechanism which produced a slow tide, until the
long lobster antennae waved under its motion.

In the morning I discovered that I had left the letters of Oscar Wilde in that flat of Avner's friends. It took me a long time to retrace my steps. Eilat is being built in a hurry: the houses follow each other wave on wave—little cubes push each other out on the dusty, sandy slopes between the sea and the steeply rising mountains. In ten years, the town has grown from a handful of pioneers into a community, and some of the growing pains are reflected in its ugly sprawl, so inappropriate to the magnificent, natural setting. It is easier to ask for particular people than for the number of a house, and when I finally found the flat, a neighbour on the landing told me that Avner's friends had set off for the beach.

All the year round, the beach is the social occasion of Eilat. There is one long stretch, rounding off the final peak of the Red Sea gulf into a great curve; the yellow nail of an extended blue finger. It runs along to the barbed wire dividing Eilat from Aqaba which nestles in Jordan as shimmering and unapproachable as a mirage. The shore is flinty and shingly but in any case there are no sunbathers under so scorching a ray, unless in winter. The water is beaten into a perpetual fibreglass surface, but as if to vindicate itself, it is always so cold that to enter it is a frigid wiping-clean of the sweat pouring down the skin. Many people put on dark glasses and a hat and stand in the sea up to their necks while the sun does its worst. Children splash around naked while their mothers lie attenuated on tarpaulins, occasionally sliding down into the sea to cool off. Bamboo covers offer them some protection against the sun, but none against the hot dry wind steadily blowing down from the Negev, spitting sand into the face, tormenting the inhabitants trapped in its line of fire between the high mountains on either side of the descending valley, the Wadi Araba.

The smart air-conditioned hotel stands just off the beach and I recognized Avner's jeep with its military markings in the car-park. The same small group of six or seven was clustered in the sea where an artificial swimming pool had been enclosed by some plastic pipes and Avner was balancing himself on their black, slippery sides, pushing off anyone else who tried to climb on, sometimes diving off himself, sometimes being pulled in by the ankle. Nobody was paying much attention except some small boys involved in the game. I asked the dumpy girl if she had seen my book, but she couldn't remember. Then I swam out across the unbroken pane glinting beyond the plastic tubes.

At lunch I learnt that Avner had taken the book the night before, having noticed that I had left it behind. It was now in his tent in the Gadna camp, he told me, and promised to take me out there to collect it in the afternoon. Among the party which had collected around Avner as usual was the beach attendant, who reassured me in German that I would get it back if Avner said so. He was an incredibly thin man, with whipcord arms folded on the table to show a series of concentration camp numbers, which had sunk a deep blue into his sun-blackened forearm. He had come to Eilat seven years ago, he said, and never wanted to go anywhere else. Unlike Avner, who expanded in response to this climate, the beach attendant was as taut as a filament, as if he had contracted himself down to essentials—the skin stretched so tightly over his face that it exaggerated his skeletal features. But he was interrupted by the dumpy girl who started to tell the whole table about the journey she was about to make on a tramp-steamer from Eilat to Massawa in Ethiopia and on to Mombasa. She was going deck-class, which meant no food for the trip and no protection against the sun, although she would be sailing through the world's torrid zone at the height of summer. It was the first time she would be going abroad—there is a heavy tax on foreign travel for Israelis which has the unfortunate double effect of restricting movements and frustrating the young, and forced her to accept that foreign travel entailed this kind of thing. One of the engineers was a friend of them all and it had been his suggestion that she should be the ship's only deck-class passenger. The lunch eventually broke up in a flurry of arms and legs as they hurried away down to the harbour to arrange the details of her passage and to fix some system of obtaining food.

Avner and I went into the hotel for a cup of coffee which we were given free because he knew the waiter. Tourists stopped to examine the khaki figure sprawling so insolently on a sofa in front of them: his army shirt was watermarked with sweat under the armpits, forming white fan-shaped rings, and his hair was upright as it had dried full of salt from the water. Boots with heavy rubber soles were thrust out at their gay beach-sandals, but I don't think that Avner even noticed their reactions in his absorption with Israeli defence policy which he was explaining to me. He belonged to the 'Ten Plagues' school, maintaining that if ever there were a real crisis Israeli guerillas could so sabotage the Middle East that pushing the Jews into the sea would have to be a suicidal operation. At last we drove off, out of the car-park sizzling with hot tar, past the landing-strip and the King Solomon's café, up to the road out of Eilat. Almost at once the landscape turns barren, swallowing all the green into its sandy plain or jutting the high-jagged redstone ranges against the blue sky-line. The mountains of Edom, rising craggy and almost purple beyond the Jordan frontier, enclose the narrow strip of low-lying desert falling down to the sea. Over the short distance to Avner's camp at Beer Ora there are few signs of human endeavour. At a bend in the road Avner suddenly stopped the jeep. A few scrawny palm-trees huddled round a broken well from which led a water-pipe: it was an old brackish watering-place for the Bedouins in the past. Bending down, Avner lifted a submachine-gun from under his seat and lay down on the verge of the empty road to blaze off a magazine over the waste. The bullets thudded flatly in the afternoon hazy with heat. There was nothing in sight and at first I was too taken aback to speak. After the bursts of firing, Avner stood up and came back to the jeep. 'I wanted to see what you'd do,' he grinned at me, 'there are plenty of ambushes on this road, it might be real.' I was angry and afraid that he might hit somebody or provoke answering fire from the other side, but he answered that they thought it was just target practice and anyhow they all knew him over there and were his good friends. He showed his strong white teeth, and we drove on, leaving a little pile of empty shell cases hot by the roadside. It was easy to see that I had failed this test of my nerves.

Beer Ora is fitted into a fold of the hills, secluded and even lost, down a track off the main road. It is something between a boy scouts' encampment, a transit camp and a holiday centre. Trees have been planted and lawns laid out to conceal and shade the wooden huts and the rows of olive-coloured bell-tents. Avner propelled his jeep into a central square which was uneven and on an incline. As he got out, he pointed out the nearby surrounding hills which were decorated with stones, whitewashed and arranged to form the mottoes of previous youth squads which had passed through Beer Ora on their pre-military training. Pausing only to explain some of them and their exploits, he disappeared into the trees, and I sat down at the entrance of a tent to wait for him. The camp seemed abandoned, except for the jeep boiling in the open square. The headquarter buildings were opposite, marked out by an Israeli flag, and after a while I walked across and found a supply of iced water available from a communal drinking fountain. Soon afterwards a corporal arrived, a girl looking cool and smart in her starched, pressed uniform and white socks, with a beret pulled down on her forehead. I asked her where Avner had gone and she took me through the lines of tents to a painted hut beyond, whose superficial disorder gave away its occupant, although it was some time before I unearthed Oscar Wilde and my notebook from under some clothes. The corporal stood watching me until I found them. In the clear afternoon I could hear orders being shouted in the valley below the camp, and coming out into the sunlight

I saw four platoons of what seemed virtually children being assembled and marched off. Avner was with them, conspicuous even at a distance with his compact figure and black beard. Noticing that they were carrying rifles, I asked where they were going, but the corporal was indifferent to such exercises which she must have seen scores of times and shrugged her shoulders. The ranks of fresh-faced boys and girls filed away, playing at soldiers with their hats like dunces' caps, their uniforms and their guns—and Avner exhorting them, an energetic games-master encouraging from the sidelines. I asked the corporal how I was going to get back, but she had turned away, and once back at the headquarter compound, she joined three or four other soldiers who had collected there. One of them came over to tell me that I could not stay, and that I should not be there in the first place, but since she proposed no alternative I went into the nearest bell-tent and lay down on the camp-bed in order to read.

'Bournemouth is delightful, and we would have long talks, on the things of Life and Art. I have just finished my first long story, and am tired out. I am afraid it is rather like my own life—all conversation and no action.' The distant shouting had died away: presumably the exercise had begun. Avner had abandoned me and would probably not return until it was too late for him to drive me back the fifteen miles to Eilat. But I had not been able to catch up with much reading before a gleaming tourist bus drove into Beer Ora, so that its thirsty coachload could gulp down some iced water. It was my cue and I mingled among them, slipping past Avner's jeep to the bus. Mopping themselves and complaining, they jostled to get at the faucets while the guide was explaining what young Israelis did at a Gadna camp, what training was involved. Some of these tourists had glared at Avner and myself in their hotel earlier in the day, but now they seemed too dazed by heat and information to respond, and I merged into the crowd, pleased to cadge the lift back to Eilat. But first the coach drove on to Timna, to

King Solomon's copper-mines, twisting off the main road down a *wadi* and along a broken track cutting through a gorge in the rocky hills. At the end of the track, two natural pillars rose against the side of a perpendicular cliff-face, and these had formed a natural blast-furnace as the desert wind fanned against them. Down there, waved the guide, thousands of slaves had sweltered out their lives. Glistening with its plexiglass roof, the coach swung round in a large arc over the reddish sand and, churning back along the track, it eventually deposited us in the car-park of the hotel. Going down to the beach to bathe before the sun sank, I showed the beach attendant my books as an excuse for being so late. The swimming-pool delimited by its plastic tubes was now empty; the sun was losing its power to burn the skin the moment one was out of the water, and a long molten gold carpet spread up the Red Sea, disappearing into the fiery umbrella over the horizon. Like chameleons, the mountains changed colour in the light, from a translucent brick-red to purple as the shadows began to fall on them. With a final little squib, the sun sank, and the darkness settled. I got out of the water, and having dried, walked home, stopping to watch the last aeroplane take off into the velvet sky. In my room, the huge insect was still baneful in the lavatory bowl: nothing could remove it. Returning to the King Solomon's café in the darkness, I sat down to read.

III

The following day I spent some time talking to Bubi, from whom I was renting my room. He had seen me at lunch with Avner, and he was critical of this group of friends. Things were now not what they had been in the old days when he had first come to Eilat, just as the road through the Negev was being completed. There had been great hopes for the new town: enthusiastic volunteers had arrived, in spite of the awful conditions. But something of a gold-rush had followed: the government had offered tax reliefs to people who lived there and this had attracted unwelcome careerists or layabouts. Bubi regretted the old world of pioneers, his friends, men who wanted to build up the town for its own sake. But goodwill and energy were powerless while the development of the harbour lay in the hands of the planning authorities in Tel Aviv. Schedules were not kept and the work was bad, with the result that the town was stagnant. Into the vacuum came Avner and others like him, complained Bubi, young toughs anxious to make the most of the unique opportunity, and to lead a life of Wild West irresponsibility, the rough-riders of the Israeli frontier. Most of his contemporaries from the first wave of pioneer settlers had already left in their disillusion and he was considering going too, for he did not want to be the last of the veterans. As it turned out, Bubi told me prophetically that Avner would come to no good. With the deadline approaching, I had to prepare my article on Wilde, and so I settled down in my room for the rest of the day, breaking the work only for a visit to the central town pump which supplied free fresh water with the local magnesium deposits removed, and to the King Solomon's for my meals. Late in the afternoon, too, I went for a swim, clambering on the undulating plastic tubes as Avner had done.

Establishing a routine, I went down to the beach at the same time the following afternoon. The beach attendant asked me if I had heard the rumours, but when I answered that I knew nothing, he refused to continue. Instead he suggested that we should go and find out: the girl was sailing that evening, and all her friends would be certainly seeing her off. Any news would have come to them. We walked round the coast to the harbour where a rusty, dirty steamer lay at anchor. Alongside the makeshift docks were packing-cases and a few idle cranes and joists. Sure enough, the group had assembled inside the gaunt and empty shed with corrugated iron sides and girders across the roof. Knapsacks and parcels of food lay on the floor around the group: two of the boys had been persuaded to accompany her, and they were all being briefed by a lanky, very dark,

Ethiopian who had himself done the journey in the other direction, to end up at Eilat. According to the beach attendant, this Ethiopian had messianic ideas, and had come to Israel to assuage his aspirations, which remained obscured, however, because he could speak only a few words of Hebrew or English with which to communicate them. Meanwhile he was employed as a building labourer. The dumpy girl had that slightly abstracted look of all travellers, as if she had already begun her journey and was coping with unexpected difficulties, and we all stood or sat awkwardly round her until the engineer came in and it was time for her to go on board. Avner was expected, and perhaps it was his absence which made her departure seem rather solemn. Rumours were apparently going round Eilat that something had gone wrong on his exercise, but nothing was confirmed. I wished the girl a good journey and slipped home.

It was Bubi who told me what had happened, standing in his scrubby, sandy garden with a gloomy scowl on his face. Encouraged by Avner apparently, six boys had detached themselves from the main exercise, which was just a night patrol, and decided to carry out an initiative test of their own, to cross the frontier into Jordan, walk over the mountain range to Petra, carve their names on a rock temple as evidence and slip home again with a piece of the famous red stone. It was quite a well-established act of daring: lots of young men were able to boast that they had done this journey successfully. But these six had been spotted on the other side and tracked down. In an ambush, three of them had been killed, although the other three had managed to escape unhurt, and had now returned. It was the most depressing incident of this kind that he could remember, and Bubi looked as if the deaths had a personal shame which was his responsibility. After all he had helped to found the new town, at a time when there had been very little trouble, especially considering how close the frontiers were, and there had even been some collaboration over camel-smuggling, and also over an outburst of rabies in the past.

I left Eilat the next day, catching a morning flight to Tel Aviv. It was a relief to see the last of the insect which still tenaciously maintained its position in the lavatory bowl. Already the heat was immediate and overpowering once outside the Arkia office. Next to me was the hypnotist who had performed in the open-air amphitheatre, and I asked him if his visit to Eilat had been a success. 'You know our good Jewish people,' was the reply in a strong Scottish accent, 'they're the worst bloody audience in the world for getting past.' And he said no more. The aeroplane swept out to sea, revealing the full curve of the gulf, shared by Egypt, Israel, Jordan and Saudi Arabia. Then we headed inland. I caught a distant sight of the King Solomon's café, at this height just an isolated little box. Perhaps Avner was there and I regretted that I had made no effort to discover the truth of the rumours, whether the disaster had really taken place. A boaster but not a gambler, Avner had not seemed the kind of man to run other people's risks. His trim beard, the exhortations to the children, the marching lines in the white glare of the afternoon; all this looked just an act, nothing to do with three dead bodies. I picked up my book: the article would have to be posted next morning. Wilde was often too disingenuous: 'Good people, belonging as they do to the normal, and so, commonplace, type, are artistically uninteresting. Bad people are, from the point of view of art, fascinating studies. They represent colour, variety and strangeness. Good people exasperate one's reason; bad people stir one's imagination.' We flew over the new town of Mitzpa Ramon, built on a plateau of rock in the Negev, and soon afterwards the whole desert opened up below in a long wide view, crystalline, regressive and accidented.

IV

In the autumn I went through the fiction of the second passport and crossed over to the Arab countries. In order to save everybody's face, I spent a long time tearing up envelopes addressed in Hebrew, and ensuring that nothing was packed up in Israeli newspaper. Even so I forgot the tags on my clothes, the trademarks on my sandals and the wrappings of my razor-blades, so that my first evening in Beirut was spent destroying this evidence. An Arab boy in the hotel who could read neither his own nor any other language, helped me make a little bonfire in the bedroom, ignited by an expensive silver lighter borrowed from a Kuwaiti businessman on the landing. Some objects were indestructible: I threw out of the window a tin of dusting powder proclaiming its Tel Aviv origin, and I like to think of security forces analysing the contents of the canister found on an abandoned site.

But it was not until I got to Jordan that the question of Israel impinged. In the hotel in Amman I was offered pamphlets to read: there was the recent hypothesis of a Jordanian member of parliament that the United Nations was a Zionist organization: a bookshop in Jerusalem contained copies of the protocols of the Elders of Zion. By arrangement I had met up with some friends who were making an extended tour in a Land Rover, and we left Amman on the road to Petra which stretches southward like a new ribbon across the bare Judean desert. It was just before dusk when we reached Wadi Mousa, the village at the head of the gorge which drops away into the ruins of Petra. Although the night was falling, we could have abandoned the Land Rover then and there and ridden the last few miles down: just below the village the pack-horses could be heard jingling their bridles. But in the police station, whose ugly fortified enclosure dominated the mud and plaster Arab houses, we were strongly encouraged to stay—the horses would stumble and throw us, we would miss the spectacular view. So we decided to spend the night in the police station, and the last pink moments of daylight were expended in argument about the price of beds, of entry tickets, of tomorrow's horses. It appeared that it was utterly impossible to drive down the tarmac road to the entrance of the ruins because of a padlocked barrier. Through all these negotiations, which were carried out in a dingy office of the administrative section in this miniature fortress, our spokesman was a corporal of the tourist police, a man who knew some English.

Later in the evening, as we were sitting in the courtyard of the police station eating the food which we had brought with us, the tourist policeman became friendly. There was a United Nations Land Rover with an Italian major and his family driving down to the ruins in the morning: 'No cars are allowed, but only some,' the policeman explained. After a long debate, we were permitted to join the convoy, as a privilege, and we were also to understand that it could be dangerous, for not long ago there had been a Jewish raiding party. The policeman thrust his unshaven chin into the yellow circle of the paraffin lamps and grinned. His front teeth were gold, and they glistened in the poor light. He could see no sense in fighting, he said, but there was no cause for raiding parties. The Jews were welcome to what they had already got, as far as he was concerned, there was room for one and all—he opened his arms to show how empty the countryside was. This had been a gang of young thugs from Eilat, he didn't know how many but they had shot them up and strapped the dead to the backs of camels, to bring them up to the police station here, in this very courtyard. It was happening all the time but this had been the worst raid, and there were several dead Jews to prove it. The bodies had been taken to Aqaba and thrown back over the barbed wire fence on to the other side so that they could bury their own people. One had to be careful down here, it wasn't like his last posting in Jerusalem which had been a much better job. We smoked our last cigarettes in silence and then crouched down to sleep in a big open room with the police dormitory overhead on the first floor. Boots clumped up and down the ladder until dawn.

In a way, the tourist policeman kept his word, for we

were allowed to drive down with the United Nations major and his family, but were then told that we had to follow him out again at lunchtime, as he would lock the barrier after him. Once in that unbelievable valley, these problems receded. It was important to do any hard walking before it became too hot, and we began with the Treasury. On the back wall of the interior hall were carved the names of previous travellers—Lady Charlotte Rowley, and her party, 1824: Edward Lear, who had signed in fear of death at the hands of his Arab dragoman. Later, on the mountain over-topping the Treasury, I came across a wall covered with Hebrew names in bold Hebrew characters, most of them written within the last few years, to judge by their freshness. It must have been something of a popular excursion at one time. Towards evening we climbed up a zigzag path to the top of the western ridge where the Deir monastery is so improbably and inaccessibly carved out of the rock-face, its ornate and baroque façade lost among the crags, although the vast ceremonial urn which culminates its classical pediment rises like a sculptured chimney-pot, visible for miles off to the initiated eye. Bedouin cave-dwellers at the top tried to sell sherds of pottery and antique glass: their goats were herded in front of the temple. Behind the monastery another range of mountains shut out Aqaba and the distant Red Sea. As we returned in the failing light, a man was walking up the path. Dressed in a uniform which had once been white, he was barefoot, with a bandolier slung across his shoulder and his revolver half out of his holster. He wore a red cummerbund round his waist and a straw hat something like a boater. Moustaches drooped down his sallow cheeks to give him the appearance of a pantomime bandit. When he passed, he raised his right hand and spoke some words we did not catch. I saw his white teeth and was irresistibly reminded of Avner. At the bottom of the mountain, we were anxiously warned not to stay out on the hills after dark. It was dangerous: there were accidents. So we spent the night at Nissim's Camp among the ruins. When finally we were ready to leave Petra, it took most of the morning to unlock the barrier, for it was a matter of finding the boy in the village who kept the key for his father, the official superintendent. The United Nations jeep had long since driven away, and we never saw the tourist policeman again.

Chapter Five

SOME ARABS

I

IT WAS IMPOSSIBLE NOT to argue with Riad, for all his conversation was designed as part of a continuing debate. Opponents were everpresent and tortuously wily—whether Israelis, foreigners, his family or friends—so that it was as if he felt compelled to guard against the possibility of being caught unawares. His dark eyes would stare out cautiously at harmless questions about the weather. His arguments too, were always a little more passionate than his thoughts, for he had a habit of detaching himself from what he was saying, standing back as it were, to observe himself and to note the reactions on his audience. At the end of some long rigmarole which covered the same ground from all possible approaches, I used to feel that he 'had gone on record as saying' whatever it might be, and, like a prudent person, made sure it was a truism. Not that Riad didn't know what he was doing; he was far too clever for that, and never likely to make such a mistake. Probably he felt somewhere in his heart that he was speaking for all Arabs, and used his brain to cover this up in case his obscure sense of responsibility should give him away.

To be an Israeli Arab is to live permanently with an inferiority complex. Riad used to describe it as the cleverest trick of the Jews that they had transferred the complexes derived from their position as a minority in various European countries on to the Arabs, as if the only way of curing the disease was to pass it on. Perhaps this was the relationship with which they were most familiar, and they felt lost

96

without it, so that they had recreated the complex by merely reversing the roles. Riad knew little of the history of Europe, and did not want to know any more, for he looked on it as a bloodthirsty chronicle which any sensible person would regret and ignore. For him, the Jews had grown collectively out of a background of centuries of persecution at the hands of Europeans, who might differ nominally but taken together were indistinguishable. Hitler happened to be German, but from Riad's point of view, he might as well have been Russian, English or French. Assimilation was a vague panacea put forward by liberals but its principle purpose was to cloud over the real issues of race. It hadn't worked there and it wouldn't work here. Many of his best friends were Israelis, but he never forgot that he belonged to the minority, and this helped him to understand the Jewish mentality. He was as obsessed by this as some Jews in the Diaspora are self-conscious and sensitive about their isolation as a minority.

The first time I met Riad, he was with his close friend, Seif, moaning about their lot, and I realized only afterwards, when I knew them better, how much I ought to discount. Certainly Riad's family had suffered. They had been merchants, or shopkeepers, in Haifa until 1948, and had been among the more prosperous of the large Arab community. Riad could remember the outbreak of fighting quite well, for he had been thirteen at the time, young enough to avoid fighting, old enough to have opinions, as the British troops withdrew to the dockside and the flag was hauled down, as the armoured cars drove down the Carmel with the Hagana commanders exhorting the Arabs not to leave. But what sort of persuasion comes along a machine-gun barrel, he would ask, would you have trusted words from a gun-turret? Then there were the promises of the victorious return in a fortnight, boastfully announced from the Arab radio stations, which they had believed. His father hadn't made the panicky mistake of running away in the little armada to Acre across the bay, and then on into the refugee camps, but had returned to his land in their village.

And that was where they had to stay, broke in Seif, because if an Arab wasn't on his property on that May morning in 1948, he lost it and so if he owned two properties, one was certain to be confiscated. That was the law, they shrugged, and there was no point in going to court because everybody knew what kind of justice troublemakers received. Besides, the Jews had to get their hands on Arab land, that was what the quarrel was about, and the war had decided who had won. Confiscation and appropriation were just as much of a legal fiction as going to court: they had lost some of their *dunams* of land near the village too. Split up into different land-holdings for a nearby *moshav*, it was now better farmed too, so it had gone like everything else, and nobody should expect anything different. Riad and Seif favoured this kind of conversation, going round and round until they became gay at the misfortune.

Riad was a schoolteacher. He had got a job in his local village which had swelled to the size of a small town. Perhaps if he were younger he would have gone to the university, but when he grew up after the war, places at Jerusalem University were even harder for an Arab to win than they are now. Also he had developed an affection for this village, nestled in the Galilee hills with such skill that it seemed to grow out of the soil, and indeed the little whitewashed houses were mostly of mud. He felt close enough to the land to be reconciled to staying. Only the aggressive cubes of the new houses, all foursquare and concrete, disturbed the harmony, and aesthetically Riad strongly resented the crude bungaloid shapes, while acknowledging that they were some token of advancement, if hardly of progress. As a compromise, the new buildings mostly remained unfinished, even if large families had already moved in, and this blended the glaring architecture more satisfactorily into the landscape. Riad knew that the old unity of the village was doomed, but he was not prepared to make a stand to defend it. I understood better what the contradictions were when one day he took me to the top of the village to look at a bunker hollowed under the walls of two old houses whose corners adjoined. The earth was held together by the thick roots of a chestnut tree which grew alongside in a small open patch of ground. In the hole lived two youngish women, refugees since 1948, who had reached this village in their attempt to flee to Syria. Against one of the broken mud walls of the houses, they had knocked together a hutch for the rabbits which they bred in order to make a living, and although the hutches were protected from the fierce sun by a piece of draped material, the rabbits looked sweated to extenuation under this shading. Both the young women, black-eyed, plump and cheerful, apologized for not inviting us in because there was no room, and through a window which was a roughly framed hole in the wall where the hill sloped away, they offered us some jellied sweets, hard and dry after a long preservation in a carefully protected box.

My own impression was that politics were ostensibly of little or no interest to Riad, and he always protested that only fools pursued politics seriously. A fastidious person, he preferred to do the things which interested him: secretly he was a dandy, and even in the hottest weather he would wear his suit and a closely-knotted tie. Aristocratic manners separated him from his friends, although they grudgingly granted that Riad had the old-fashioned Arab courtesy, while Israelis tended to take his politeness for sarcasm. Occasionally, he would explain, he had to descend into the market-place and occupy himself with politics because it was expected of him at this time when nearly all Israeli Arabs remain inarticulate. His involvements in politics had been mostly unsuccessful, and brought about by his friends and admirers. Seif was a journalist too, which made it harder to abstain. Arab nationalism, still a confused force, and especially in Israel, demanded the participation of all educated men, if the Arabs were to rise above their centuries-old degradation. Once he had written an article attacking an Arab member of the Knesset, and as a result a gang of thugs had come to look for him in his home village.

Fortunately he'd been warned in time. It was impossible to say who had tried to beat him up, whether informers among the Arabs, or Israeli nationalists, or Arab nationalists hoping to bluff the Israeli authorities, or Israeli sympathizers among the Arabs trying to stage a false incident in order to arouse public opinion. Literature was Riad's passion, and he had all the dedication, the laziness and the neurotic certainty of a man who wants to write. His English was good enough to read poetry, and he hoped to do to Arab poetry what Eliot had done to English, to take a long, almost stultified tradition and reorientate it in the contemporary world. Modern Arab poetry was petrified in its antique metres and conventions, he said, while Arab prose was hardly worth the name. It was very much harder to achieve anything in Israel because all Arab writers and intellectuals, such as they were, had fled during the war, and literature in Israel had to start again after this clean break. Apart from the official paper in Arabic, there were few places to publish, and books were out of the question unless one were prepared to be sponsored and subsidized by the Histadrut. Riad also complained about the absence of an audience. Naturally it was impossible to reach the outside Arab world upon which his future really depended, and which would be able to judge him according to his merits, and of course the corollary was true, that he was out of touch with contemporary Arab writing. It was not much good writing for illiterates, which included most of the elder generation left in Israel: nor for the half-dozen Israeli Arabists who were anxious to seize on anything approximating to Arab culture and inflate it to prove that the Arabs were culturally independent. The logical outcome was either to write for himself and to circulate manuscripts among his friends, or to switch to Hebrew, which was what he did whenever he felt more pessimistic or poverty-stricken than usual. He had collected three or four shelves of the classics in paperbacks, and arranged them in the bookcase so that they formed the central feature of his flat. This collection, all thumbed and annotated, was a measure of his devotion to 'the great champions of freedom,' or some such phrase.

His flat was in one of the modern buildings of the village. It had been put up too quickly and with cheap materials: the walls were cracking, the plaster had spread out in uneven surfaces, nothing was quite as it had been intended on the drawing-board. Yet there was electricity and gas and running water, and modern furniture of a utility model but serviceable and even comfortable. On one wall hung a tapestry, a brightly coloured and presumably mass-produced reproduction of a stag, vaguely reminiscent of Oriental patterns, but crudely designed and woven. If he had wanted, he could have lived with his family whose house was at the other end of the village. He took me to this traditional Arab home, a ramshackle crop of one-floor rooms built on top of hard earth around an enclosed yard which served as a farm for a cow or two, a few goats and some chickens. Riad's father was always away, and Riad would explain that he was looking after a small store which he had opened, but Seif had told me that the old man had never recovered from the shock of losing his property in Haifa, and would spend the day drinking coffee with his few old friends, occasionally complaining, mostly staring into the distance and telling his beads. His mother ran the house and family, but invisibly. It was a promise that next time I should be introduced to his mother, but just now she was busy and would be embarrassed, for she was old-fashioned in her ways and not used to meeting strange men. Personally Riad wanted to break down her resistance and would ask for time to prepare her for the meeting. Still, I never met his mother, never even caught sight of her in a house which consisted in all of perhaps four, or at most five, separate rooms. At meals which she had cooked her children would serve. Different brothers and cousins turned up in profusion, talkative, excitable, eager to try out their hard-won English. The guest room, which was also Riad's bedroom if he wanted to sleep there, would be crowded by a whole group of young men in white shirts and grey flannel trousers, filling the chairs spaced out around the walls. None of the younger generation wore the traditional Arab clothes. Occasionally they would give up the attempt at twisting their tongues on the English language and instead switch on the huge radio in the corner and we would listen to dolorous Arab music. The radio is for listening to Nasser's broadcasts, one of the cousins once said with a wide smile: generally they were too polite or too circumspect to offer opinions, but if I criticized, they would criticize, or if I praised, they too would praise. And afterwards there were walks to other houses in the village, where cups of coffee would be offered, and the conversation would soon be in Arabic, leaving me to stare round the bare rooms and the shabby furniture.

Besides Riad, the only man in the village who was prepared to express what he felt as intransigently as he wanted was the headmaster, who was responsible for the school and therefore was Riad's superior. One afternoon, when the school classrooms had emptied, I was taken by Riad to see the buildings and the facilities. They were pitifully inadequate, even bearing in mind that under the Mandate there was nothing at all and the nearest educational centre was some miles off. Still, this was an important village and by no means all of the children could be adequately accommodated into the existing school which was actually an administrative building dating from the days of the Mandate and which had merely been converted into the school. Riad's classroom was an external construction of plywood and rough plaster, and on the wall was a notice-board which had this prize-winning English essay pinned to it:

Philip Reis lost his father when he was still a very young boy. He spent all the time of his boyhood in an educational establishment where he was raised and schooled. His teachers soon realized that Philip was a very able and talented boy. He excelled in natural sciences and in mathematics. When he had finished elementary school he was advised by his mathematics teacher to continue his studies in a technical school in a nearby town.

But Philip was an orphan and had no money. He had no means
of paying for further schooling. He had to seek employment—
and go to work. He went to work in a paintshop. His employer,
Mr Birbach soon realized that he is a very clever boy for there
he did not make him work too hard. Philip now had time to read.
When Philip earned enough money he left his work and became
a student in a trade school.

In the school laboratory Philip made many experiments and
invented all kinds of instruments. Among other things he invented an instrument called THE TELEPHONE which means to hear
from faraway. In the year 1861 the twenty-eight year old teacher
exhibited his invention at a meeting of great scientists and men
of learning which was held at the University of Frankfurt.

At the bottom of this essay, its twelve-year-old author had
written in thick red pencil, 'Never say Die. Up Man and
Try.' Perhaps he had caught some sentiments still lingering
in the building—the last remnants of colonial lore—but
Riad told me that the boy was preoccupied with Israeli life
and from the internal evidence, he deduced that his pupil
was studying the best way to start his own career among the
Mr Birbachs of Israel. As I was copying the essay down,
the headmaster walked into the classroom. He was a thin,
grizzled man, slightly bent, but rather as a spring might be,
as if he would snap up at any moment. His mouth was tight
and angry, a venomous button in the centre of his face. Yet
he had some of the same aristocratic aloofness as Riad,
although in his case it was almost disdainful. His family had
been rich and powerful in the district, but they had all fled
to Jordan at the outbreak of the war, and he was very
conscious that he was the last survivor. Even if there had
been no war and no state of Israel, he would have been a
fierce and articulate defender of the traditional Arab way of
life, and in the present circumstances he had the blaze of a
man at bay, driven to extremities in spite of himself.

His house was some few hundred yards from the school,
along a dusty path which was one of the principal streets.
It would have been quite impossible to drive a car or lorry

into the centre of the town. In the old days there had been camels and camel-drivers, but these had vanished. Transport was now mechanized, although the peasants still kept their donkeys for daily use. Walking through an Arab town or village usually attracts a crowd of small, dancing and shouting children, but on this occasion nobody paid any attention. For a moment we stopped to watch a woman baking her flat bread on the charcoal ashes inside a bakehouse so small that there was only room for her to squat down. Next to this little oven, a wide wooden staircase led up to his room which was the upper floor of a handsome old house. It was his only room, for he was a bachelor, but it contained a large bed, a refrigerator and plenty of chairs. In a short time these chairs were filled with half a dozen solemn old men, the village *mukhtar* and the elders, who had come to listen to the schoolmaster explaining their predicament, although it was doubtful if any of them could follow his English. They sat immobile, slowly passing the beads through their fingers while the schoolmaster's voice filled the room. He was fifty, he said, and never in the years he had lived through had things looked blacker, even through the war and the shootings and the riots and what he called their betrayal by the English, for now he and all his friends in the village were living out a death-sentence without hope of reprieve. How could he bring up children to be educated Arabs if they weren't going to live in an Arab civilization? They were expected to work and live in an alien country, and under alien masters, and yet cling to their traditions and culture although these no longer had any meaning. A Jewish state struck at the roots of Arab life, and even if the Jews should encourage the Arabs to develop their own cultural independence, it would be like the Americans keeping their Red Indians in reserves. They had been emasculated, rendered null; they might as well be a minority kept on for the folklore experts. It wasn't any use turning his children into little Jews because they weren't Jews. But it wasn't any better bringing up little Arabs because nobody

wanted little Arabs. The Jews weren't intolerant or vicious
—there were some injustices in the military government,
but not much worse than the British—they just didn't want
the Arabs, so he made sure his pupils knew it and always
recommended boys of school-leaving age to cross the
frontier and stay on the other side if they could. It was
better to remake life as a refugee in an Arab country than to
be a second-class citizen belonging to a minority which was
denied the rights and advantages of Israelis. No blame
should be attached to the Jews for their past history, he was
intelligent enough to understand that survival took priority
over any rights for other people: there was nothing else for
it, and that was what made the Arab position so intolerable
for him. Quite properly, the Jews saw that the Arabs were
a security risk; he was himself a danger to security, he added
with a unique flash of wit. And it should not be thought that
he resented Jews as such, for they had introduced many
excellent things into the country. He welcomed doctors and
scientists, he admired the schools they had built for themselves and their efficient organization. Unfortunately all
these reforms could take place only at the expense of the
Arabs who could not develop freely in so different a culture,
and the Jews were so assured of their own superiority that
they ignored Arab cultural and psychological needs. I
interrupted him to point out that the standard of living of
the Arabs from all sections of the community had risen
immensely, but economic solutions did not satisfy him.
Piped water in the villages was not much use, he said, if
it kept peasants even more bound to the land—where they
could not compete with Jewish agriculture—as if by new
chains, and anyhow this new prosperity merely blinded the
masses to their real deprivation. There was Riad, once his
prize pupil and now just an underpaid schoolmaster: he
knew of a physicist who couldn't be trusted in this country
because any research he did might involve a security risk,
so he had emigrated to America instead and had found a
university job. His big brown eyes, sunken into his head,

were malevolent with frustration. There was nothing for it, he reiterated, except to drive the children across the border. Bitterly he added that there was nothing the Jews would welcome more: the problem was now beyond a solution, and the clocks couldn't be put back.

Darkness was creeping over the hillside and we sat in the shadows which obscured the passive faces of his audience still clicking over the beads in their hands. The hot evening glow turned to pale velvet. Three miles away was the border; only an Israeli border patrol and a rusty strand of wire held them back from friends whom they had not seen for fourteen years. Lights came on in the houses around, animals were grunting outside and chickens squawking, children playing in the dust, a woman still baking bread in the tiny communal oven. A man riding past on a mule cried up a greeting. More friends crowded into his room up the wooden staircase, sombre old men like himself, some in grey or brown suits, others in Arab dress: it was time to go, and we gravely said good-bye. As I thanked him, he invited me to return and stay with him so that he could explain the situation more fully. I could sleep in his bed and he would move out on to the balcony. Only after a day's talk could we really get to the bottom of things, and he looked forward to it.

In the open spaces of the village, people now gathered round to see who we were. A woman offered us the flat bread which she had just made. The night was heavy with the distinctive aromatic smell of Arab villages, of cooking and herbs and eucalyptus trees and dung, compounded all day under the sun. Two hours ago we should have gone to visit a friend of his, said Riad, but never mind, the man would still be waiting. We found him too, as we continued this tour, a huge hulk of a man in his vest and pants, so vast a shape that he seemed to squeeze himself out of his compact modern house which might well have been set down in an English housing estate without causing surprise. It turned out that this man was a former Arab employee of the British colonial police, which helped to account for his bullet-

shaped head and hair clipped to the roots, the brawny arms
and sagging stomach. He too spoke good English, larded
with colloquialisms and police phrases. Now he was a clerk
in the local administration, dealing with Arab income tax:
a marvellous job, a bit of all right. With a sly nod, he pulled
out a bottle of whisky from behind a bookcase which was
full of yellowing papers and journals, and his expression as
much as declared that free whisky was among the perks of
his job. When he had filled glasses for us, he left the room
in order to put on a shirt and trousers, and while he was out,
his wife peeped round the door to have a look at us. When
he returned, he told me stories about the good old Mandate,
when a beating-up and a little third-degree were all in the
day's work. Riad said that when he was in the mood this
man could tell stories to make the blood curdle. A laugh
rumbled like wind out of the clerk's belly: he looked like
a seedy Brigade of Guards sergeant. I tried to draw him out,
but he was too careful, immersing himself in the whisky.
Not long after, Riad and he were deep in an Arab conversation, the guttural sentences rolling on and on. Later Riad
explained that this former policeman was the most influential man in the village on account of his job, and he made
full use of it to build up his fortune. Everybody was
frightened of him because of his past, and because of his
access to official documents now.

From the ex-policeman's house, we walked back into the
centre of the sprawling village. Over the humped silhouettes
of the Galilee hills there were twinkling lights, while in
the village there seemed to be more animation than by day.
The men gathered out of doors to drink coffee, squatting on
old packing-cases or some broken-down chairs. In the air
was the steady whine of Arab music. Riad took me to some
cousins of his, who also lived in a modern house, but when
I remarked on this to Riad he said that it was a disadvantage
because these houses were paid for on a mortgage and the
pound had been devalued since the contract was signed
although the money had to be paid at the old rate. This

house was very pretty though, with jasmin already growing up against it, and with a well-kept garden in front. Indoors, there was the same tapestry of the stag, but the rooms were very sparsely furnished, although the floors were expensively tiled. We sat drinking coffee, until a couch was brought in and prepared with a blanket. Then Riad and his cousin retired to another room where I could hear them talking until I fell asleep. When the household woke up at five o'clock the next morning, Riad had gone and the cousin explained in broken English that he had returned to his own flat. I offered to carry the couch back to its proper place, but was told that it would be taken care of. I never met this cousin's wife; but I shook hands with the cousin and discreetly left, slipping out past the scented jasmin, sharp in the clear dawn air. The peasants were already working the fields in the valley below.

II

It was difficult to find out much about Riad. Surface information was easily available, because he was something of a phenomenon, and gossip gathered round him. People claimed that he was a communist, a Mapam Arab, a Nasserite, an informer; Israelis could be made to run the whole gamut of possible guesses. All agreed that he was an *againstnik* of some kind, and the hardest case to make out was that of his indifference to politics and his desire to write poetry instead. I was assured that the security forces would have him filed and that perhaps I ought to be more careful before associating with such friends. The schoolmaster in particular sounded like a suspicious character. All real evidence however, was nebulous, but it was incontestable that if any of these Arabs had been trouble-makers or dissidents, they could have been deported from the village and sent to live in some other part of the country, under one of the regulations of the military government which obtained in that part of Galilee. Other regulations would have allowed the authorities to restrict their movements and confine them to certain selected places, reporting regularly to the police as a safeguard. But Riad had his pass, although he treated it with contempt and rarely carried it. He boasted that on any bus or in any area where he might be stopped and questioned, he would be certain to speak better Hebrew than some policeman from Tunisia or Morocco, too slow-witted to learn the language as well as he had. Indistinguishable from the next person, unless through the neatness of his invariable suit, white shirt and tie, nobody could have decided if he were Jew or Arab. 'I'm more Israeli than any Israeli,' Riad would often say, as if this were sufficient comment.

Once I asked him point-blank if he were a communist, and he answered that, as I suspected, he had never belonged to any political organization, but he could see that I had been talking to Jews, who could never believe that people sometimes avoided joining the parties and political organizations which cut through every level of the country. At the time we were in Nazareth, accompanying Seif to the house of some friends, but at the crucial moment when Riad was explaining his lack of affiliations, he broke into Arabic in order to argue with Seif. In the back streets of Nazareth, there was little or no sanitation and we had to walk close to the walls in order to avoid the filth stagnating in the stone-course down the middle of the cobbles. Water-melon skins and decayed vegetables floated in the puddles of flaccid water, giving off a swampy smell throughout the crooked, close-built *souks*. After pausing for a moment to discuss what they ought to do, they turned under a doorway and we walked across a shaded courtyard into a room which was cool behind shutters, and at that distance from the street, clean and whitewashed under a high vaulted ceiling. Eight or ten young men were sitting round drinking coffee and ceremoniously we shook hands with all of them. Unless Riad or Sief translated for me, I was unfortunately unable to understand their conversation, but apparently it was considered that as a foreigner and a writer I should be allowed to stay, so that I could obtain a true picture of Arab life.

Nasser had just made a speech on the wireless, I gathered, which had stirred them, for he had announced more or less simultaneously a new socialist charter for Egypt and that he had no immediate plans of any kind for the Gaza strip refugees, who would have to sit it out because he saw no alternative. That they were all enthusiastic supporters of Nasser was easy to see. Obviously he appeared to them as the only Arab leader of stature, and a man who might possibly be able to rescue them from their present plight. If Nasser had been in power in 1948, Seif said to me, there would never have been such a fatal partition and war, and there would have been no need for the state of Israel. The Arabs had been betrayed by their feudal kings who had been prepared to deal with the Jews, he maintained, and that was why King Abdullah had been murdered. He was the biggest traitor and also the biggest dupe for he had bought blank or dud ammunition from the British who wanted the Arabs to lose the war in order to re-establish their imperialism through the agency of the Jews. Nasser had always pointed out that both Jews and Arabs ought to stand firm against colonialism; perhaps one should not blame the Jews too much for their part in this intrigue, for wasn't it a fact known throughout the world that the Jews were the oil which ran the wheels of capitalist America? At the time the Arabs had not been clever enough to grasp this, but Arab nationalism was now fully grown up.

I asked him what effective steps ought to be taken, if this were all true. All the feudal regimes must be overthrown, Seif emphatically listed them: then the Arab people would be liberated. Within a socialist framework, Arab nationalism would find the best means of becoming operative. Once the resources of the Arab countries were properly utilized, Arab power would be evident to the Israelis. Did he mean that the Arabs would drive the Jews into the sea when this day came? He did not think that would be necessary, although most of the others in the room held that it was indispensable, he said. Some of them lived and worked only for that moment, but he believed that things would revert to their old positions, with the Arabs in sole control of the country, which would by then be incorporated into a wider Arab unity so that the Jews would assume their former role of minority subjects. Most of them would not like this, especially after a taste of power, and would go back to America where they had come from, or where they ought to be. There would be no reprisals, just the usual confiscations and that sort of thing, what the Jews had done to them, only this would be a rightful restoration of property. Nasser was a civilized man. Of course nobody could say what the extremists might do, nor some of the refugees who had been rotting in the camps all these years. The parallel, he said, was with the Crusaders, who had occupied the country by force, until this very force brought the opposition together to eject them. This might take time too. One of the greatest weaknesses of the Israelis was to be threatening from a position of apparent—because temporary—strength, when they ought to be making concessions, especially if they wanted concessions in return one day. Arab dissension would cease as their countries were developed, and then the disparate balance of power would be revealed. It hardly mattered when; a century or two made little difference one way or the other.

Meanwhile the others in the room were arguing. There was a constant, almost formal, movement from chair to chair as if they were regrouping themselves. The debate, I discovered, concerned the new community centre in Nazareth, built and equipped at great expense with American money, but deserted and even padlocked because nobody within the Arab community could agree on the choice of a director to run it. If the aim of this centre was to prevent young Arabs leaning towards communism by providing them with capitalist amenities, then they thought that the padlocks should stay. On the other hand educational facilities were going to waste. But the crux of the matter seemed to be that the rivals for the post of director came from the two principal families of Nazareth, and neither could get support for his election at the expense of the other. A compromise candidate would have been an insult to both.

This handful of Arabs was probably the nucleus of any activists who might stir up the Arabs to do something. They had been the impetus behind the publication of a newspaper, *El-Ard*, which had been so outspokenly Nasserist and anti-Zionist that it had been closed down by the government after only a few issues. They had staged successful demonstrations in Nazareth and the other Arab centres against the military government and the discrimination which this involved, and against other abuses and injustices, particularly one notorious occasion when three Arab boys had been shot dead near the frontier by trigger-happy Israeli police. The discussion over the community centre was still continuing when Riad and Seif made a sign to me, and we left the room. One of the others followed us out. As we turned back into the street, I suggested that not much political action of any value was likely to be organized if a group of like-minded men could not agree on an appointment which could only be to their advantage. Riad had taken no part in the conversation—his eyes looked sleepier and more languid than usual—but he now asked me what I would recommend them to do. They were too polite even to protest when I tried to make some suggestions, but the passivity seemed even more hopeless than any objections. The other man who had come with us said that there was nothing for it but to eat *gefilte* fish, learn Yiddish and dance the *horah*. Perhaps then they would be Jewish enough for the Jews.

We sat in a large high-ceilinged café off the main street of Nazareth. It was a halting-place for the tourists on their visits to the supposed fountain of the Virgin in the precincts of the Greek Orthodox church. Guides were to be overheard telling of the Virgin's visit to this well every day, to fetch water like any Arab woman today. Holy mementoes, rosaries and medallions, were on sale in booths around, and a huge stall occupied one side of the café. Tourists picked their way through the little trays, fingering olive-wood boxes or the plaster statuettes duly consecrated by the bishop, and haggled over prices.

Flies buzzed thickly round our table, settling on to the grubby cloth and on to the brown rims of the cups. We talked slowly, in lowered voices, as if the words dragged; sometimes there were long silences. Riad thought that there was nothing to be done except wait: revolutionary newspapers would do no good, most of the population couldn't read them anyhow: demonstrations fizzled out in the absence of specific grievances, and the Arab *malaise* was the result of their isolation from the general stream of life in Israel. The Arabs had lost their sense of identity, their confidence: he too wanted to be left alone and allowed to get on with his own things. They could be revived only by new contact with the Arab world, and this did not seem likely in their lifetime. I said that Nasser did not seem to accept this, but they shrugged—he was too clever a politician not to know the truth in his heart of hearts. Supposing too, that Nasser did lead a successful attack on Israel, they would be considered Quislings for their former quiescent acceptance of the Jews, and their failure to organize an underground. Meanwhile the quarter of a million Arab peasants deluded themselves that they were better off because their foodstuffs fetched higher prices on the market, but since there was no alternative, maybe this degradation was the only answer. Energy expended was just a loss. We ordered more coffee and the flies could now mass round the heavy-lying sedge left at the bottom of the finished cups. The other man with us began to complain about the missionary or proselytizing attitude of the Israelis, who had no respect for the Arab way of life. Hospitals and irrigation and tractors were all the Jews valued, so that progress to them was just an accumulation of material phenomena, a mastery of technical detail. If the Jews had their way, they would enchain the whole Arab world by misapplying their scientific knowledge; they talked only about sending their doctors and engineers and teachers to colonize the Middle East and could not understand that they might have something to learn. I pointed out that the Arabs did not have to accept any encroachment of the sciences which they did not want—it was their decision after all—but in general underdeveloped countries at the moment made it one of their aims to obtain assistance. But it was the didactic mentality of the Jews which was at fault: they could not see how important it was that in Damascus there was the best coffee in the world.

'The Jews should learn good manners,' said Riad. After another cup of coffee, the talk was still turning in the same orbit. It was time for me to leave, and saying good-bye I walked out of the café, past the stalls parading the holy trinkets, and I was aware of the brown, sombre eyes of the three Arabs following me, distressed and resentful at this interruption of the protracted hours.

III

On the several occasions when I saw Riad after this day in Nazareth, he was distant and even more formal than usual, as if by chance I had trespassed into some preserve which it had been his duty to protect. Not that there was anything concrete to hold against him, for his demeanour was still outwardly as courteous and self-consciously charming. Yet the contradictions in his character seemed to have risen more to the surface. A hard and reliant centre must have ensured his survival, even if this had been problematical, and also given rise to his fiercer sentiments. Aloof politeness mingled uneasily with resentment. But on one occasion we found ourselves together in the house of an Israeli friend in Tel Aviv and I arranged that Riad would come to my flat in Haifa and show me some of his poetry which we might then translate jointly, if this were possible. Nothing happened for some time after this, though, and as these were the hottest weeks of the summer, I stayed on the balcony of my flat and tried to get on with my own work.

When Riad arrived late one afternoon, it was clear that
he had brought no poems. He was his usual neat self, with
that cautious expression on his face. I mentioned his poems
but he did not want to talk about them. After a roundabout
introduction, he began instead to complain of the difficulties
of obtaining girl-friends. No Jewish girl would go out with
an Arab, he said, except for a few sluts whom he would not
want to take out, because most Jewish girls felt themselves
to be racially superior to Arabs, even if the more sensitive
of them phrased it differently—more educated or more
Westernized. To be patronized in this way infuriated him
as much as anything else in Israel, particularly when some
girl was condescending to him out of pity or a sense of duty
that she ought to be nice to Arabs. It was only another way
of saying that she didn't like Arabs but was too cowardly
or ashamed to say so aloud. No Arab girl would go out
with him because it was against everything in her cultural
and social heredity. To be seen in a public place with him
would be an insult to her and to her family and there might
be ugly repercussions. Buying his flat had taken all his money
and he could not afford to pay the bride price so that he
could not get married in the traditional way, through the
arrangement of the parents concerned. In his village it was
impossible to be on any terms with the girls. They lived
their separate existence, as if in another place, and could only
be glimpsed fetching water or labouring in the fields or
doing some domestic work, restricted to each others' company. In the cinemas showing Arab films, the men went one
side and sent their families the other, so nowhere was there
any possibility of the same sex relations as Jews enjoyed
with their girl friends. Sometimes he was able to find a girl,
neither Israeli nor Arab, to go out with him, as it might be
an American or European visitor or a secretary working
in Tel Aviv for a foreign firm, but this was rare.

The change-over from an Arab to an Israeli way of life
had imposed on Riad an unwelcome chastity which was
conspicuous by contrast with Jewish morals in the new

society. His only prospect lay in finding some girl as emancipated as he was, and among Arab women, with the many additional handicaps of their inferiority in the Arab scheme of things, this was improbable but not impossible. He did have a cousin, he revealed, who was all that he could hope for, since she was also a schoolmistress, had been educated at a Jewish training centre for teachers, spoke some Hebrew and was altogether exceptional. In the village she wore Arab clothes and did the work expected of her. If she were to pass Riad in the street, she would kiss his hand as a mark of respect. There was no question of paying her even the most formal of visits, although he had made his feelings known to her, and indeed to most of the village. Apart from the sophistication of the girl which would make it hard for her to settle down with an Arab peasant whom her parents might wish on to her, all other considerations showed that this would be a suitable marriage. The girl was away teaching most of the time, and Riad was often on the point of going to find her and propose. Yet in spite of his education Riad did not have the courage to defy the conventions, and he made no direct attempt to speak to his cousin. Through a mutual Israeli friend—the man who had introduced us in Tel Aviv, as it happened—he had arranged to meet this girl in his house, which was in a prosperous Jewish suburb where they ran no chance of being recognized. The friend promised to be out at the time, so that the two of them could have the whole house to themselves. When the day arrived, Riad told me, all went according to plan; the girl was ready to see him, quite understanding and approving of the manoeuvre. She was wearing a tight skirt and a white blouse which gave Riad his first impression of her figure. Perhaps this was too much for him, or perhaps it was the consciousness of doing something so alien to both of them, but when they were at last able to meet face to face for the first time, they were overcome with shyness and had nothing to say to one another. Both of them were shocked by their presumption, and so made a little polite conversation which was acutely embarrassing, for they were both self-possessed people. Neither of them was protected against the possible consequences of this meeting, and the risk they were running was certainly large. Marriage might now be out of the question for the girl, for she had dishonoured herself and the family. Riad said that he felt like a man shot into space with the knowledge that the mechanism was faulty somewhere. If they were found out, they could not return to the village, and instinctively they both spent the time peeping out of the window, pretending that they were admiring the garden and the thick hedge between them and the road. After half an hour the cousin got up to go and, blushing even in her silence, she disappeared down the street as fast as she could. The last glimpse he got, said Riad, was of this pretty girl waggling her behind as she trotted off, and he could hardly believe that she had been raised as a peasant in a Galilee village. Yet he knew that after such a humiliation they couldn't bring themselves to meet again.

We sat on the balcony of my flat, looking over the bay of Acre. It was no good explaining to him that a government was not ultimately responsible for the virginity of its subjects, for he clearly believed that this particular frustration would not have happened but for the state of Israel, for in the old traditional society the courtship would have been arranged without this farce. I asked him what happened when an educated Lebanese or Jordanian wanted to marry a village girl and so brought about a similar clash of attitudes. The girl's family would be flattered that she was marrying a man with decent prospects, so that there would be no problem, he answered, and anyhow there was no parallel between the cases, for in Arab countries the whole society was changing from top to bottom, but in that sense at least it was homogeneous, while here it was more than a question of pace, it was also a comparison with the different standard which the Jews went by. In a way, he envied them their sexual freedom.

After we had eaten supper, I invited him to spend the

night on a camp-bed on the balcony, but he insisted on catching the last bus home, so I drove him down the steep hill spiralling to the bus centre at the bottom. All this suburb of Hadar Carmel hadn't existed when he was a child, and he used to climb up through the pine trees and the gardens of the few villas mostly owned by Englishmen in the administration. He wanted to have a flat of his own in Haifa one day, and fill it with girls. Under the fluorescent lighting at the Egged station, I arranged a date with him, when I would spend a few more days in his village. And meet his mother—without fail, this time. And perhaps translate some poetry: he noted it down in his diary.

IV

It was from Seif that I heard the news of Riad's brother, who had attempted an escape to Syria, had been caught on the frontier and was now in the hands of the Israeli police. We were sitting on the same balcony with its spectacular view, just as I had sat with Riad. This flight had come as a surprise, for the brother had hitherto shown signs of wanting to accommodate himself to Israeli life, and Riad had done everything in his power to help him, which made it all the more bitter. At sixteen, the boy was apparently quite clever but lazy. He had complained to Riad that there was no point in going to an Arab school if he were to live in a Jewish state, and through Riad pulling strings, he was transferred to a Jewish school. His Hebrew was already quite good, more advanced than that of the new immigrants who attended this rural school. It had cost a lot of money to send the boy there, for it had also entailed living away from home. Perhaps this had led to loneliness, for he was unhappy and complained of discrimination and bullying. Most of his energies were absorbed in this schoolroom struggle and soon he wanted to return home, so Riad arranged that his brother should work in the school where he himself was a teacher. Here he had come under the influence of the old schoolmaster who had worked on the boy's imagination with his stories of Arab life and civilization in the past. This boy was another victim of his master's advice. It was no adventure, no liberation to cross the frontier, but merely an illusion of enterprise for any refugee was bound to be captured. It appeared that the boy had evaded the Israeli border patrols, had crossed into Syria and was picked up by soldiers as he was making his way across the open country. A few hours later he had been handed back to the Israeli police on the frontier, considering himself fortunate not to have been treated as a spy. Since then he had been held in custody.

Riad had been to see him, but was too anxious about his own position in the affair to want to help, and too annoyed that his efforts on behalf of his brother's education should end like that—especially through the agency of his former teacher. I remembered the fanatical face explaining to me how important it was for the children to grow up in an integrated Arab society, listened to by the elders while the children played around in the streets below, their laughter and shouts coming up into that upper room. There was something worse, though, Seif went on, Riad had been suspended from his job. A letter had arrived from the ministry some days after his brother's escape, announcing that Riad's services were no longer required. It must have had some connection with the flight, although it gave no explanation, and Seif maintained that Riad had been framed. He suggested that the brother had tried to run away but had been caught by the Israeli police before crossing into Syria. The authorities had used this as a pretext to dismiss Riad who was a potential menace to security because of the following of young intellectuals who admired his work, but still they would not have dared to remove him from his job without some grounds. I said that the brother would give the game away because he would tell the truth, that he had been captured in Syria and handed over to the Israeli police, but Seif argued that the boy was quite stupid and it would be easy to confuse him, to shout at him and move him in a closed transport from one prison to the next, until he came to believe that he had crossed the frontier and had been handed back. Nothing would come into the open for a long time because under the regulations of the military government he would be tried before a military court without right of appeal. Nobody could say for how long he might be detained, and meanwhile Riad had lost his job, for he could not answer the ministry that he was not responsible for his brother's actions when he did not even know if these were the grounds for his dismissal.

I saw Seif several times during the next fortnight, for he was greatly overexcited and spent his time travelling round to his friends to convince them of the injustice done to Riad. His theory had collapsed for Riad had seen his brother and it emerged that the boy had gone into Syria and been handed back, but Seif was still sure that the accusations were put-up. Certainly the boy admitted that he had planned to make his future in Syria because he was unhappy in Israel and had finally decided that he could not live there. The connection of the escape with Riad's dismissal was too strong for Seif to abandon, and temperamentally he wanted to overdramatize. If he were right, however, this was a moment to make a protest in his newspaper articles and I urged him to do so, for it was an ideal opportunity to expose unfair and discriminatory treatment. From Israeli friends I could discover nothing. This kind of incident was trivial, it was happening every day, boys ran away to Syria because their teachers were fool enough to stuff their heads with dreams, and were then surprised when the illusions came home to roost. Talk finally ended in action, but Arabs did not like to recognize it: that was what security forces and the military authorities were for. One incident more or less made very little difference, for the reality was that all Arabs would be unnatural not to hate Israel and it was better to accept this fact, and countenance an injustice or two along with survival.

The matter could be solved only by Riad and I wrote to him to say that I still looked forward to coming to his village but would understand if things were now too difficult and he would prefer to cancel the plan. I received no answer but through Seif I heard that Riad would come to lunch the following Friday as we had arranged and then we would drive off for the weekend. I would have another chance to talk to the schoolmaster and ask him what he thought of the double disaster. I waited for Riad until late in the afternoon. About an hour before sunset, I went down to the beach to bathe, certain that he would not come, but leaving my bag still packed in case he arrived, and a note pinned to the door. He never turned up, and indeed I never saw him again. I wrote a second letter, posting it to his village to ask as tactfully as possible what had happened. It was never answered. And I saw nothing of Seif either, until the last time, when I called at his house. His sister and her family were living with him during their holidays and there were so many people in the two tiny rooms that I could hardly talk to Seif. He told me that things were just the same, he hadn't written the articles because there was too much risk, and there was nothing he could do. He hadn't seen Riad for a long time now but he knew that he was all right, having moved into his mother's house in order to let his modern flat and receive a rent for it. With nothing to do all day he was bored, but trying to write, and perhaps he might translate some English classic into Hebrew. The brother was still in prison: they'd all given up trying to help him, and Riad was determined to let the boy take all that was coming. Unexpectedly my patience snapped: I couldn't bear the big talk any longer and got up to go. As usual it gave Seif offence that I was leaving so soon after arriving, but for the first time since I had known him, I gave up trying to be conciliatory when he started the routine sentence about Europeans being in a hurry. I no longer tried to anticipate his feelings and compromise what I was saying, but rudely answered, 'If you want to get anything done, you'll have to get used to European ways, won't you?'

Chapter Six

ERNA AND JOSEPH

I

DURING THE HUNGARIAN REVOLUTION, when the secret policemen were being hounded down the streets of Budapest or were lying dead in their high-collared uniforms and jackboots, and so were indifferent to the fate of a single family, Joseph and Erna walked across the frontier and on to Vienna. Their daughter, Rosa, was nine at the time, her life-span fitted into her parents' release from the camps and this new uprising. Not that Rosa minded the walk to Vienna: it was exciting, if a little straightforward because nothing happened on the way. They merged into the stream of refugees. In Vienna, an Australian visa was the easiest to obtain. No strings needed to be pulled, there was none of the lobbying which surrounded the American and even the Canadian consulates. One place outside Europe seemed much the same as another to Joseph. All their possessions were in two suitcases which could be unpacked anywhere. They accepted Australian visas and set off on their journey to Sydney. Since their adolescence, for one reason or another they had tried unsuccessfully to shake off Europe: it had clung to them like a malignant disease.

Neither of them was particularly happy in Sydney. It was difficult for them to explain this dissatisfaction: perhaps Joseph resented working in a factory instead of as a goldsmith, or Erna minded the drudgery of the government stationery office where she typed every day, to maintain their large budget. They had enough money though, for the first time in their lives, a flat luxurious by comparison with Budapest, an untrammelled existence free from the past and the miseries of Europe. Erna rationalized the unease into boredom, but probably because she did not stop to examine the basis of their lives. Joseph had become phlegmatic about the circumstances in which he found himself, so long as there were the minimum liberties. Rosa grew up in this detached suburban atmosphere.

It was Rosa's education and her future which decided them to leave Australia. Or so they claimed afterwards. In an admission of candour, or a throwback to a more secure memory, they agreed that they did not want her to be brought up in this world of Sydney where she would almost certainly marry a gentile, and finally lose her identity, and theirs. Yet it had been to achieve something similar that they had emigrated to Australia and hoped to start a new life. Nostalgia perhaps, or prejudice, burgeoned in the security of their existence. Neither Joseph nor Erna were specially conscious of their Jewish religion: they had merely come to realize that after what they had been through, they wished to bring their daughter up to know what it meant to be a Jew and the only place for this was Israel. To satisfy this need, they went to the Jewish Agency to arrange their passage, and so for Rosa's sake, they broke off the slender connection with the New World.

Erna was one of those women who complain as if they were saying their prayers, a repetitious pattering under their breath. There was nothing to complain about in Sydney, nothing specific to look forward to in Israel. It was typical that shortly after her arrival in Israel, she was heard saying that there were too many Jews around. One of the reasons which she publicly maintained for leaving Australia, as if to save face, was that she couldn't go to the cinema on a Sunday and this had irritated her. Plumpish, no longer young, her mouth was now mostly a flash of gold and shiny false teeth, and she had reached that age when this complaining had been absorbed into her routine. It took the place of a transistor radio. On the boat they had met an Uruguayan professor of mathematics who was emigrating to Israel with his family. The three small daughters carried huge South American dolls, gaudy and gold-spangled, so that Erna was sure that these were little statues of the Virgin Mary and had tried to pick a futile quarrel with this wholly agnostic don. Nor was Erna any politer or friendlier to the North Africans also taken on to the boat at Marseilles. It was all for Rosa, however, and Rosa should know it. Joseph kept quiet: he had long ago given up so simple a delusion as holding expectations for the future. Sallow and thin, he spent the journey staring down at the blue flecked water.

Arriving at Haifa, they were separated from the mass of immigrants who clustered forlorn and fraught under the vast corrugated iron roof in the customs' shed. The professor of mathematics and his family were driven off in a black car to the job already awaiting him, although first he would have to spend three months learning Hebrew in the high pressure of an *ulpan* designed for professionals. Alone of the other immigrants, Joseph and Erna had volunteered through the Jewish Agency to go to a kibbutz, and so they were escorted to a Land Rover which was standing by for them, while the North Africans, many of them too old and infirm to understand the proceedings but shuffling along in their traditional robes in the direction which the Agency officials directed, were detailed off into the transport lorries which were to take them to a designated *moshav*. Minutes later, they were out of the docks and travelling along the wide streets of Haifa.

They had been allocated to a kibbutz near the shores of Lake Tiberias, but since neither of them had much conception of the country's geography, it made little difference which settlement. The rapidity and the change of landscape bewildered them both, and they felt slightly cheated that the arrival had been so simple, and so unceremonious. Furthermore Joseph's sister-in-law, their only relation in

Israel, had not come to the ship to meet them. Only Rosa, bumped in the back of the Land Rover, retained some of her curiosity, staring out at the scenery, first industrial, then giving way to farm land, and finally to the mountains circling the still blue surface of the lake.

When they drove into the kibbutz, the secretary met them and escorted them to their house. As a privilege because they were newcomers, Rosa was to sleep in the house with them and not with the other teenagers. Later she could decide when she wanted to move over. The secretary's wife arrived to show them where everything was; most of their possessions were provided free by the Jewish Agency but as they were settling on a kibbutz, they required less than most new immigrants. The conversation took place in English until a third person, also a Hungarian, turned up to interpret. When Erna had unpacked, she began to ask how she was going to fit the radiogram which she had brought all the way from Sydney into this small house, to complain of the cupboard space, and the size of the beds. The Hungarian cut her short, to her annoyance, and advised her not to try that kind of question in any other language, for she almost certainly would not be allowed her radiogram in this kibbutz. Erna nearly burst into tears. It was time to go to lunch, however, and after the short meal, the group went round the kibbutz while the Hungarian lectured them about the way of life and the organization and the purposes of the various buildings. By the time the tour was finished, Erna and Joseph were so depressed by what they had taken on, that they almost decided to leave for Tel Aviv and find their sister-in-law.

When I met them on the kibbutz, they were still finding it hard to become acclimatized, for their expectations had been vague and unformulated—except for their hopes for Rosa's future—and the life contained nothing familiar or enviable. They were conscious of being the rejects of Europe, unable to settle in a stable existence after so much disruption. Such convictions as they could identify in the other inhabitants seemed to them strange and remote, and in the absence of convictions, the people were either peasants or trying to find refuge from an even harder way of making a living. Neither Erna nor Joseph had much patience with the pace of this agricultural existence which filled up the day but did not satisfy them. Nor could they learn Hebrew with much speed. To learn English in Sydney had demanded an immense effort and readjustment which it was exacting for them to make a second time. Rosa, however, picked up the language with great fluency, and in a matter of months she was speaking and reading it. Going to school every day, even though with children younger than herself, gave her more opportunity. It was with an air of condescension that she spoke to her parents in what was now a foreign language to her, and in turn they were rather humble at not being able to follow the daily details of her life with her new friends. Erna told me that this had been the first important estrangement between them, aggravated, of course, because Rosa took some pride in her proficiency.

More important for Joseph was the fact that he could not adapt himself to the work now required of him. There was a plywood factory on the kibbutz and Joseph was sent into it, on the grounds that he would be more suitable there than in the fields. The unskilled work which he was given bored him and the intimacy and the pleasant surroundings were matters of indifference to him: the finished products were too crude for him to obtain any of the rewards he had known in his old profession, and in the back of his mind he consistently hoped that he would be able to resume his trade as a goldsmith. So after six months in the plywood factory, he wrote to his sister-in-law, asking her to find out discreetly if there might be any jobs available for him in Tel Aviv. Erna was aware of his dissatisfaction, but felt that they had reached the end of the road, that there could be no going back, and indeed there was now nowhere else to go. So it was in her own interest that she began to temper her criticisms. They were naturally being watched very closely by the members of the kibbutz, who wanted them to settle down and be happy, and I was later told that as Joseph became more restless, so Erna had grown more accustomed and more silent. By nature more observant and hard-working than he, she tried to find the pulse of the life here. It eluded her because like Joseph, she was offended in some reservoir of prejudices and assumptions about life which her character depended upon, and which were opposed to the anonymous, indiscriminate life of the kibbutz. She had always clung to the belief that self-assertion, even gentility, mattered, and was enforceable. Here it plainly counted for nothing, and once Erna understood as much, she was in a position to defend herself rather more effectively. At her work she was competent enough, although unused to such hard and continuous effort. Nevertheless the impression which she made on me was of a wariness and a determination; I noticed that Erna set about her daily tasks in a different spirit from the other women.

At first Rosa was interested and shy; which in many ways is a better approach to a kibbutz life. The other children of her age accepted their life as normal and found it difficult to conceive of any other. Their ignorance amused Rosa: she was able to show off too; her knowledge of languages, and her travels. Experience came to her through schoolroom chatter: there were new things to learn, but she had as much to impart. But the first serious blow came when the secretary suggested that Rosa was now ready to leave her parents' house and move in with the teenagers. There had already been complaints about this, and he explained how rapidly jealousy could spread on so controversial a point. Allowance had been made over the radiogram which they had been permitted to keep, and it was impossible to make too many concessions. Erna and Joseph refused to let Rosa go, they disapproved of boys and girls of this age sleeping in the same rooms, taking showers together and starting affairs too easily, so they held out until Rosa took the decision for them and moved her things over to the teenagers' house.

The rupture upset Joseph more than Erna, for it attacked his authority and undermined his sense of the fitness of things like family hierarchy and obedience, settled things which he clung to all the more passionately in that all his life he had been forced to fight for survival against the destruction of such values. Perhaps only the knowledge of certain quite primitive beliefs and emotions of this kind had enabled him to survive the forced labour camp. He understood that bringing up children in a kibbutz involved their living communally but was somehow unable to refer this to himself. Rosa's departure seemed to negate all the reasons for his emigration to Israel. When I first met Joseph, he was like a man who had been quite deflated, but the explanation usually given by the *kibbutzniks* was that he was temperamentally melancholic. All talk with Joseph concerned the impossibility of having family life as he knew it on this kind of settlement. Not that he saw much less of Rosa, nor that she had been given a sudden access of freedom, but just that he could no longer control the private daughter-father relationship which he valued. Also she was now an accepted member of a free-thinking society, in essence little different from the gentile world of Sydney which he had deliberately abandoned. At about this time, too, his sister-in-law wrote that she did not know how to set about finding him work, but she enclosed some money so that he could travel and look for himself. Since the kibbutz allowed him the equivalent of ten pounds a year, this money represented liberation, and he hid it under the floor of his hut and waited for the opportunity to go to Tel Aviv.

Movement was restricted from the kibbutz. Situated right on the Syrian border, under sharply rising hills, there was a limit to ordinary walks. Sometimes they would go as far as the river Jordan, whose stream flowed gently and prettily through nearby fields, bordered by willows. There were the rare expeditions to Safed or Rosh Pinna: the children were taken on educational trips to Tel Hai and the early settlements in this part of the Galilee, and as newcomers Erna and Joseph were allowed to accompany them. Otherwise it was too remote a place to have dealings even with the flanking kibbutzim. A further restriction on them was the road under construction along the very border, on an escarpment in the Syrian foothills. It was designed to facilitate communications, and was a project of the Keren Kayemet, the land development agency. From the beginning there had been shooting, none of it very serious or dangerous, but sufficient to keep the members of the kibbutz in the underground bunkers. Spasmodic firing would break out unexpectedly, directed at the bulldozers and heavy equipment on the ridge, but since the kibbutz lay under the line of gunfire, there were alarms which slowly became integrated into the routine. But because it was accepted so calmly, the tensions played on Erna and Joseph who had hoped never to hear the crack and whine of a bullet again. It seemed that late one afternoon the firing broke out more violently than usual—sitting as I was in a comfortable deck-chair in the kibbutz listening to the story, it was hard to visualize the interrupted peace. People went down to the bunkers with the air of phlegm which they generally adopted but there was a rumour that somebody had been killed, one of the road-builders or a sentry. When Rosa did not appear, her parents began to worry and Joseph set off to look for her, although this was against orders. There were communicating trenches to all parts of the kibbutz and Joseph made his way underground, for although the firing was not aimed at the settlement, it was passing overhead. There was no sign of Rosa in the teenager's quarters. Joseph was about to go to his own house when he caught sight of somebody moving in the shower-bath next to Rosa's room. Entering, he found Rosa taking a shower with a boy, both of them disregarding the warning bell which should have sent them to the underground shelters.

When he had confronted her, Rosa had shown no sign of shame or embarrassment: she took it as quite natural, and explained that they always took showers together, but perhaps she was fonder of this boy than of the others. What especially upset Joseph was that this boy was a Tunisian. David was dark-skinned, with big black eyes and a large nose, and very foreign-looking to Joseph. Furthermore he was a boy of some education, who came from a poor family only too glad to be rid of the boy on a kibbutz. When he went to the secretary, he received a lecture on the importance of not raising barriers between the sexes and allowing the children to be uninhibited. Joseph lacked the courage to say that he did not want his daughter to meddle with a dark-coloured North African. To make it worse, David apparently came to him once, and talked very lengthily about the disadvantages of being North African, how he was despised for the shading of his skin, and was only fitted for manual jobs now that he had missed the chance of a technical education. To Joseph's amazement, Erna was not very sympathetic. True, she was angry with Rosa for throwing herself away on the first *kibbutznik* to come along, but she maintained that when one was in a place one ought to accept and adopt its customs. Admittedly, North Africans weren't very nice, but he was a good Jewish boy and that was what Joseph had wanted. Of course, it just depressed Joseph to admit that he didn't want *that* kind of Jewish boy. It decided him to hurry on his plan to leave the kibbutz.

I was at the kibbutz again when one weekend he took the money under the floor and vanished. Erna made no reference to his disappearance, no questions were asked, but it was obvious to everybody. During his absence, Rosa came to her mother to say that she thought she was now in love with David and he had shown her what a kibbutz life could really be. Erna came to ask my advice, on the flattering assumption that I might know if a girl with Rosa's Australian background would fit into a kibbutz. Meanwhile too, I had met David, whose ambition appeared to be to write a book exposing the handicaps of North Africans in Israeli society. He was highly precocious, and I thought he intended to leave the kibbutz if he could be assured of further education. After three days Joseph came back, offering no explanation. None was required of him. Erna's mood fluctuated a good deal at this moment, for she sympathized with Joseph, who stood for all her values and prejudices, only he had the courage to express what she preferred to conceal, or delude herself was a process of transformation. Assimilation was a criterion to Erna but to Joseph it was natural to assume that every man's hand was turned against him. Joseph stayed on the kibbutz for a day, during which he once more told Rosa to drop the boy. On being disregarded, he walked out, taking the radiogram with him, and moved to his sister-in-law's flat in Tel Aviv. The radiogram was a pledge of his intentions. For days the kibbutz talked of nothing else.

II

People were embarrassed at discussing the whole affair in front of a stranger like me, although I could pick up the main currents of opinion. It was accepted that Joseph was not kibbutz material, and that it was a good thing for this discordant and stubborn man to leave, even though nearly everyone felt a measure of guilt that the kibbutz had been unable to accommodate him, and they did not express their feelings quite so callously. On the other hand, Erna was suitable, for her lingering prejudices would clearly be broken down in time and she was anxious to establish herself. Rosa had obviously taken to the life easily enough. Since she was no fool, Erna perceived this general attitude. She resented feeling that the kibbutz supported her while rejecting Joseph, but since she badly wanted to be liked and accepted wherever she was, it also weakened her resistance, and succeeded in putting her into a state of mind in which she could take no decision. It was unthinkable to abandon Rosa to her boy-friend but her own past and future belonged to Joseph—too much common experience dictated her emotions.

At first sight I had taken against Rosa. At the time she had been helping someone with the housework, busying through their room, fingering and prying in that friendly way which is no more than condescension. She was a tall, gawky girl, sallow like her father, with her black hair done up into a floppy bun. Out of her shorts, which she rolled up right to the top of her thighs, came a long, sunburnt pair of legs, and in a way, she had a good figure. It was likely that the affair would not last long—and Erna also thought as much—for she was both bumptious and unsure about David. But as opposition developed in Erna, Rosa became more blatant, and she used to lie in the evenings on the grass in the centre of the kibbutz showing herself off with David, treating the place as a theatre in the round, well aware that she was being observed. 'La Dame aux sabras,' I once heard someone say. In the close atmosphere of a kibbutz, shyness is easily smoothed out into brashness or disdain.

I do not think that after her months on the kibbutz Rosa had any feelings stronger than friendliness towards her parents, but a new certitude that her life was now her own to mould. When Erna at last came to her senses and ordered Rosa to obey, to pack her clothes and leave with her at once for Tel Aviv, there was the inevitable row. It took place in Hungarian, so nobody could understand what they were saying, but the neighbours quickly sent for the man to interpret, who came hurrying along to listen from the garden at the back and translate for the curious eavesdroppers indoors. Rosa had some of her father's characteristics, for she was quite impervious to arguments, and Erna at least had the consolation of abandoning her daughter in a furious temper. When I saw her briefly, she was trembling with frustration and resentment at being thwarted. Her farewell shot was an interview with the secretary when she accused him of conspiring to wreck her marriage and kidnap her daughter. Erna's rupture was complete.

Later, I heard that she had found Joseph with his sister-in-law, made amends, and organized his life in about a week.

They moved to Jerusalem where Joseph found work in his old trade as a goldsmith, and they found a flat in a street inhabited mainly by Hungarians, so they were able to take up the former threads of their Budapest life. Only the radiogram was left behind in Tel Aviv as a proof of bad management. Walking by chance in the streets of Jerusalem on my last visit there, I met Erna and we had a drink in Fink's bar. It was more her surroundings than the kibbutz dining-hall, and she seemed to have expanded now that her character was allowed its free rein. She had taken a job at a printer's, and quite soon now she would be confident enough to start negotiating with the kibbutz about Rosa. I was able to tell her that before I had left the kibbutz, Rosa had become the complete Israeli, in her cotton clothes and small hat like a dunce's cap fitted on to the top of her head and pulled down in front over her forehead. Voice, mannerisms, habits of thought, were all being transformed. I had warned the secretary that trouble lay ahead, that these were not the kind of parents to let their daughter go without a struggle, especially after all they had been through, but he was not interested in my opinions, and had answered that it was a great pity that the kibbutz had been unable to hold on to Erna, she was a wonderful person, a real pioneer, and her presence would have kept Rosa in place. To her credit, Erna was very angry, and as we emerged from Fink's on to the hot pavement, she was promising that Rosa would not have it all her own way in the future.

Chapter Seven

GERMAN AFTERMATH

IT WAS A QUARTER to four in the morning when I was
woken up by somebody shouting my first name outside the
hut. This was a procedure I never got used to, especially as
it was difficult to break off conversations and go to bed
before eleven or twelve the previous night, so that only the
imperative demand not to be put to shame could prevent me
falling asleep again. In one sense it was a rewarding experience though, for during the summer months, there was a
quick pink dawn in the Negev, shedding a young light
whose tenderness gives no indication of the coming cruelty.
Until about six in the morning there is a heavy dew on the
ground, lying wet as rain. As I had to be ready to leave for
work at 4 o'clock sharp, there was no time for a wash,
except to rub my hands over the thick grass in front of the
hut and wipe my face with the fresh dew. In my open
sandals too, I could wash my feet by dragging them along
the ground and then wriggling the drenched toes. When the
sun rose, this dew glistened as if the earth had been covered
with a silvery cobweb. Then it steamed briefly and was gone.
By eight o'clock the heat of the day was well established, and
any greenness left in the grass or the gardens would be
jaundiced by the long crescendo to noon.

There was the first feeling of wonderment at being up in
the crystal dawn, with one or two others in sight, slipping
through the trees towards the dining-hall. Cups of tea or

coffee and bread and jam for the hungry could be had in the kitchen. There was nobody yet at work at that hour in the kitchen and so there was a feeling of raiding the larder for any scraps. For a few moments we could sit around, edging on to the tables and piled-up chairs, or pushing to grab the food. Boots resounded on the lino floors, nobody spoke unless it was a curt good-morning, as if still trying to shake off their sleep: we would sit in a circle of unshaven chins and stale-smelling clothes. Outside the tractor and its trailer or the lorry would come crashing and grinding along to collect us and by a sort of general assent, we would put down the mugs and all pile on. Generally there were stragglers who ran behind and jumped up on the tailboard. One tall, dark, disjointed but very athletic young man from Iraq would make a particular habit of timing his over-sleeping so that he would catch the others up at the last moment before the lorry lurched off towards the fields, and swing himself on board with the ease of an acrobat, then settle down to yawn all the way to work.

It was easy to begin work with a sense of anticipation which was undiminished each day. The landscape of the Negev is mysterious with unfulfilled promise and devastation, so that cultivation only intensifies these contradictions, especially the awareness of the long to-and-fro struggle between sand and soil. The northern part of the desert consists mostly of good earth permeated through the centuries by sand and salt. Its flat and rolling aspect makes it something of a tundra, appearing to stretch for hundreds of miles. Patches of green crops and orchards are like little quilts fitted in here and there, arresting the eye with their strangeness. Brown dunes carry on the view, rising to break the monotony, to create shallow folds. In the winter the rains collect in these folds and sometimes even flood, but the returning sun only dries out the moisture to leave the surface brick-hard as before. Occasional Arab farms, the mud shell of a building or the mausoleum of an Arab sheik, its small dome now stoved in like an egg-shell, cluster round the sparse springs of water, sustaining a palm tree and some coarse grass or reeds. In the south where the desert becomes mountainous and wholly forbidding, the black tents of the Bedouin are almost the only resistance to nature in this wilderness.

But as we jumped off the trailer and began to work in these cotton-fields, or vegetable crops, or orchards, there would still be the refreshing cool drops of dew to splash on to our hands. At first, too, everyone is still in a straight row, hoeing or weeding or picking together. The scratch of trowels or the bump of fruit into a wooden crate is comfortingly close. Slowly the workers drift apart: some trees are barren, some lines of cotton are choked with weeds, others are clear, and so a strain of competition enters the morning, together with the first strong flush of the sun. Pink and gold and radiance have disappeared. Why has the bearded man who was alongside at the start now thrust himself out a hundred yards ahead of the others? Only the chunk of the young girl's mattock behind to the left reassures against an inferiority complex. There is the suspicion that one is being secretly observed, that one's energy or clumsiness is the subject for comment—for here there are no norms or standards of production and only the approval of others guarantees a respectable place in the community. It is a relief to hear the girl expressing her irritation at hoeing a row which has grown only thistles, and the man next to her turns back so that they attack together in a frenzy of chopping.

Here too we are next to the largest air-base in the desert. Its runways are secreted out of sight and almost out of mind over the distant sand. But fighter-bombers are suddenly overhead before one can straighten up, and the jet whine is splitting the eardrums only when the aircraft have swept their wings low over the horizon. We are all peasants, straightening up to gaze at these new wonders of science and shaking our heads over the screaming interruption to the peaceful morning, to our private world whose axis is the row ahead. Once bent back at work, there is nothing to think about except the thin stalks of the cotton plants, flamingo pink and easily cut down by an awkward or over-enthusiastic swing. Weeds grow in the hothouse climate of the nights and days like tropical plants and these fields have to be scraped clean almost twice a month. Or else there are the spiny twigs of the pomegranates, scratching one's arms and bare legs, while the ripe fruit stains the fingers with its royal red dye. And the peaches, warm and palpable as flesh, but difficult to reach in the thickness of the trees. After eight o'clock it is already too hot for comfort and the dew has long given way to sweat. One finds comfort where one can—endlessly repeating the word pomegranate, or thinking of Persephone who should not have eaten one. It is time to be with the others, at more or less the same place even if it means skimping a little work and even though they may have covered more rows—one must not be conspicuous. Even the strong, bearded, stripped-to-the-waist pioneer young man has had enough and has the self-confidence to shout out that he is bored and, throwing down his trowel, he sits down beside the ditch and offers a good enough excuse for a gossip. By unspoken agreement, people wander off towards the waiting lorry. It is breakfast time.

In a washroom just outside the dining-hall, there are a couple of basins, and we queue for these. It is a pleasure to stand up and jostle after the contortions of the morning. The towels are muddied black before we are all sitting down to our food. By contrast the women, already settled at the tables, appear particularly clean and well-dressed, although most of them have also been at heavy work in the kitchen or the laundry. The separate tables for four or six people are rapidly filled up. Trolleys come round and men or women who have not been at work in the fields serve the food—the fried eggs and *lebanya*, or yoghurt, tea and fresh milk. Vegetables are already on the tables for us to make our own salads: stainless steel bowls are provided for the slops— there is an atmosphere of vegetarian efficiency and natural health about the meal. After the intensive four hours of work, breakfasts usually take place in rather earnest silence, for most people are concentrating on the serious business of eating a large meal. All too soon it is time to go out once more to the tractor and back for another three or four hours to finish the day's work. Eating is only punctuated, then, by the plop of cucumber peel into the bowls or by a request for more food, unless there is somebody of garrulous spirits at the table. With the briefest of interludes, we resume where we left off. The heat of the day is far more excessive and taxing for this second period, and a greater amount of energy and will-power is called for to achieve less results. Instead of the dew to greet one, there is the sun-smitten dust off the desert: not the radiant dawn but an implacable copper. As one begins again, the work seems insurmountable, but gradually a rhythm imposes itself, and at some point one discovers that this rhythm has taken control, immersing the mind and body in its regularity. Pain lies in interruption—the back almost yells aloud as it is straightened, the head spins off as one wipes the sweat away, to stop it pricking the eyes. This immersion is perhaps the equivalent of a vocation for after a while it is easy to feel dedicated, swept away by vacuity—it had nothing whatsoever to do with any romantic theories of labour, which appeared derisory if one ever stopped to think about them. Again the work would come to a halt sometime after midday, by the same kind of common consent, and there would be another collective amble back to the lorry askew in the corner of the field. There would usually be a short while to wait before lunch—during the heat of the day which comes shimmering off the Negev—and most people would make haste to plunge into the swimming pool. (This pool, incidentally, was built only a few years ago, financed by the German reparation money due to one of the members of the kibbutz. He gave all the money for this communal pool and the members dug it out during their spare time at weekends.) After lunch, there would be a siesta and the day would decline away in an anti-climax of leisure, unless there were some seasonal demands, an urgent harvest, a farming emergency, crops to be sown, or some internal work to be completed. Volunteers might be found mowing the lawns or tidying flower beds. Otherwise people pursued their private interests, sat about and talked, or read, and recovered their energy. There was always a slight feeling of lassitude and falling-off about the rest of the day: breakfast was the watershed; once the crisis of the work was over, the calm verged on dullness.

It was at breakfast that I first met Dieter, when he asked me how I was getting on. We had a routine conversation about the unfairness of the weeds which took advantage of piped irrigation to grow faster than the cotton. I could see that he was highly-strung and the impression of nervousness was accentuated by his rapid but inaccurate English. Most of the men around us spoke English, although some were unwilling to put their school lessons into practice. As a matter of retaining one's identity on a kibbutz, the choice lies either between letting go completely in an extrovert manner, or remaining rather reserved. I was a follower of the latter 'new boy' school but I was familiar with Dieter's face because in no time at all, the faces of the kibbutz become part of one's mental furniture. It is even possible to arrive at some reasonable estimate of their characters without ever speaking to them, for when everyone is engaged in the same things at the same time, questions of value are simplified. On this kibbutz there was a *Nahal*, that is to say a group of friends volunteering to do their military service on the land, which seemed to provide most of the motive force of this settlement. There were about fifteen of them altogether, more or less of the same age, and all of them *sabras*, or born in Israel. Different in size and colour and appearance, they nevertheless formed a cohesive unit and so stood slightly apart from the rest of the community towards whom they were even a little condescending, which they could afford to be because their position was only temporary. Equality does not cover strength, nor output of labour which depends on muscles, and certainly these men were privileged in their physiques. It was hoped that they would choose to stay on the kibbutz after their national service was completed—this is one of the avowed aims of a *Nahal*—but most of them were restlessly impatient to be on their way. Dieter worked with them and at first seemed to belong to the group. I rather mistrusted a close-knit *élite* of this sort, and so I was never very curious to find out his exact standing among these prefects, although I realized that he was a hanger-on. He seemed a slightly weedy, insignificant figure who had attached himself to these large protectors and I could remember many examples of this behaviour from my schooldays. His lanky frame was certainly out of keeping: so were his almost comic snub-nose and the acne on his face. Strong brown legs with a lot of curly fluffy hair were more appropriate.

I could see that Dieter was making the first overture at friendship—it was the usual development in a kibbutz where newcomers are first absorbed as units in the daily routine and kept under watchful but distant inspection, until they prove their worth to the community whereupon the barriers are broken down by the forced advent of friendship. Intimate friends are made in a matter of minutes, once this initial acceptance has been approved by an old-timer, an already established resident. But one inherits enmities in this way too, and after months on a kibbutz it is still possible never to have spoken to somebody and yet feel his hostility. It is easy to understand how unwanted or unsuited people can be driven away—not by anything dramatically said or done but by the permanence of these barriers. It is a great relief to the volunteer when individuals suddenly burst through and offer their friendship. By the same token, the relationship which *kibbutzniks* most miss is that with the person they like but do not see enough of—a common enough form of friendship in the outside world which avoids the all-or-nothing extremes. Soon Dieter was coming to my hut in the evening, as the day cooled and gracefully admitted its failure to boil us alive. It took me no time to discover that, like myself, he was not an insider of the kibbutz. What he wanted was a neutral observer to discuss it all with him, because the *Nahal* overawed him too much. There were other foreigners on the kibbutz—notably an American and an Italian who in the cotton-fields would try to argue about communism or freedom, much to everyone's annoyance—but Dieter had rejected them because he wanted to make sure that he would be taken seriously. His was a mind quite incapable of conceiving a joke: a light turn of phrase sent his forehead wrinkling down towards his snub-nose to decipher all interpretations of it. He could be made to laugh rather as a bird can be made to speak—a throaty, rattling invention to cover up a disability.

He had his reasons. Dieter had come to Israel four months before with a goodwill party of students from Cologne. They came with highminded intentions of making amends, and to this purpose they had sacrificed a vacation and a part of a term. As far as I could understand, most of these young Germans had enjoyed themselves in Israel, where they had worked with keenness, travelled round the country, admired what they had seen, and gone home pleased that they had contributed towards it. It had given them a new view about Jews, and one that they were satisfied with, all of them except Dieter who was rather revolted by this superficiality. The clue, as he confessed, was that his own father had been a well-known Nazi journalist, a political columnist, a man who was now employed as a broadcaster and had made a reputation since the war. It was the central fact of Dieter's life: he was all the more eager to tell me because he felt unable to unburden himself to others on the kibbutz. They knew he was German, and they knew why he was in Israel, but if they were to penetrate to the secret and realize what kind of column his father had written—Dieter would fall silent. He had a habit of using high-flown language, obviously transliterated into English. But the abstractions failed him all too often and he would sit miserably brooding, hating the facts of his youth and upbringing.

One afternoon, it seemed, when he was about thirteen, his father had taken him for a walk in Düsseldorf, the nearest city to the Rhineland farm where the family had lived out the end of the war. Those years Dieter remembered as rather exciting, the tanks and the marching soldiers, the nights flared by tracer shells and searchlight. The hours spent in the farmhouse cellar were the only contacts with his family which stayed fresh and permanent in his mind. In all innocence he had accompanied his father down the devastated Königsallee in the centre of Düsseldorf. One-floor shops ran down its length, displaying inaccessible glittering objects behind the plate-glass: cameras, electrical equipment, household gadgets. In the rear, the piled rubble often topped the flat roofs of this long rash of make-believe shops, and often the shopkeepers were still living in what remained of the old fabric, a surviving room or a basement. Dieter's father began speaking of the war, to explain why the city had this appearance. Things had got out of control, this was apparently his key phrase. That afternoon the boy learnt the whole story as his father saw it—walking past these shops of black-market show-goods, mocking the hungry street-walkers. Dieter told me that it was as if walls had suddenly arisen in which he was to live for ever, he was aware that nothing would be the same again for him; it was a conversion. A single remark of his father—'It was so right'—remained with him vividly. When it was uttered, they were having tea in the wealthy and arrogant hotel rising out of the ashes at the bottom of the Königsallee.

His father made no objection when Dieter announced that he was giving up his vacation to work in Israel. The father could still hurt but not command. The young party of Germans was directed to Dimona, a new town growing in the most uncompromising location, stranded in the wastes of the Negev on the plateau above the Dead Sea. It has almost every inconceivable disadvantage, geographical and climatic, but it may prove economically viable if it can serve as a labour centre and social service for the Dead Sea chemical plants at Sodom, and the nuclear research station not far away. For six weeks Dieter and his friends had carried bricks, dug sand and laid foundations, driven mechanical equipment, mixed concrete, until it was time to return to the university, when Dieter in his obsessive way refused to leave Israel until he had contributed something of his own and felt that he had understood more of the historical problem. So he had moved to a kibbutz in the neighbourhood—at least by the standards of the Negev—and there I had met him. Outwardly he continued to associate with the young men of the *Nahal*, sticking close to them at work, swimming with them, taking off his glasses in order to wrestle with his friends round the edge of the pool, determined and pedantic, assimilating with them. But after our first meeting, he would come round to my hut in his spare time, during the hours of siesta, so that if I wished to avoid him I would have to borrow the hammock of the man who lived in the other half of my hut, and sling it at the far end of the garden among some secluded pine trees. It never offended Dieter: *Sturm und Drang* was so much a part of his nature that all cause and effect merely drove him deeper into himself, another searcher in the long-drawn German hide-and-seek for a soul.

My hut was in the old part of the kibbutz, dating back to its foundation in 1946, when a group of soldier-pioneers had dug in at this strategic point in the Negev, in anticipation of the coming fight. It was called the Vatican, taking its nickname from the Hebrew *vatikim*, or old-timers, and in contrast to the newer part of the kibbutz, built in the last few years, which was known as Sweden. In essence the hut was a crude construction of planks and hardboard, thrown up in the shape of two rooms and a shower. My room, the smaller of the two, was hardly more than a cubicle, and its two gaunt bed frames with their streaky blue-and-grey mattresses left only a narrow alley down the middle. The mosquito wiring across the window was torn and the walls

were therefore scarred with the victims of bloody encounters.
There were no cupboards and no drawers—only a plank
nailed as a shelf—for life in this hut required no place to
store possessions. In the other room beyond the thin plywood partition lived Israel, one of the old-timers who had
founded the kibbutz: there were only four of them left.
During the first few years he had lived not in the hut but
in a bell-tent, or a bunker, for they had been attacked when
war had broken out. Dug in on the only spur for miles round
in the flat desert, the defence had not been hard, but they
lived under constant fear of running out of food or ammunition, for there was no possibility of relief in their isolated
post. The kibbutz had consolidated into an agricultural
rather than a military community, and Israel had built his
hut with his own hands, so that now he refused to move
into the more comfortable accommodation available to him.
He was a greying, withdrawn and melancholic man who
succeeded in leading a private life of secrecy under the
constant observation and interest of his hundred or more
colleagues. Perhaps through the prestige of being a founder-
member, he had convinced them that community life was
elastic enough to absorb a lonely eccentric who disliked
interference. There was something of the hermit about him:
his asceticism and aridity belonged to the retreats of the
Essenes and the cave-dwellers of the Dark Ages. What
Israel did with his time remained something of a mystery,
but it was even more mysterious that he was allowed to
keep himself so aloof and undisturbed. Except for playing
his gramophone in the evenings he made no sound at all,
not even through the plywood so flimsy that to kill a
mosquito was like firing a gunshot. I think that he probably
sat in his chair and slept away his life—certainly he worked
as if his intention were to erode himself. It appeared that he
had spent thirteen years in Paris, with the conviction that
he was a great painter. A modest existence came to a stop
with the realization that he had been deluded about his
talent. He never painted again, threw up his studio, and

came to the kibbutz without so much as a drawing to substantiate his past. Work, laborious and methodical, was his chief standard and pastime. Paths and flower beds were incessantly relaid and weeded, until the garden was bare with his exertion. He was always getting into difficult postures in trees so that he could lop off a dead branch. All round our hut were small piles of wood which he had squirrelled together and which he consumed in winter to heat the antique and rebellious boiler which gave out more sound and fury than hot water. Israel's face was placid, with that ironed-out complexion of people who have done what they wanted, come to important decisions and stuck to them in the belief that they were right. Grey hair neatly brushed, cloudy eyes; his face was always arresting with its mixture of illusion and reality. Israel had authority. All the time I shared his hut, I never saw the inside of his room. He never invited me in. I never went in by myself and would never have followed the general kibbutz habit of calling on him: it would have been an impertinence.

Privacy, however, depended on our thin partition. Israel must have overheard every word that Dieter spoke in my room. He made no comment. We greeted each other with the usual reserve and occasionally exchanged polite conversation in French—almost the only discernible concession to the studio in the past. It was very unlike most other relationships and friendships on the kibbutz, where reserve is not a quality to flourish: it is quickly mistaken for hypocrisy. Although people do not pry into each others' lives, unavoidably they are aware of the tensions surrounding them. A kibbutz is suspended and vitalized by a close-spun net of gossip, gossip not in a malicious sense but as a means of information and communication. Hence it is the *cri de coeur* of *kibbutzniks* that they have no friends, that they know each other beyond the stage of confidences and intimacy, to a point where they are differentiated only by minute details of work and domestic arrangements. Thus relationships in a kibbutz are ground down to gossip because the larger, more vital aspects of life, their circumstances, hopes, beliefs, financial straits, are common to one and all. Nobody alters or develops in the day-to-day framework in so pronounced a manner that it can be commented on at a higher level than gossip. Old age, the death of love, the hardening of sensibilities, the ripening of friendships, all touch people at so many points that they are perceived only as trivial details of life, in the cowshed and the kitchen. Rhythm is all-important—the long slow pulse of different humans from different backgrounds determined to live as one. If the chart shows violent ups and downs, the community is disrupted and, unlike an individual, does not regenerate strength. Emotions are, and must be, sacrificed to the common good. Behaviour is none the less eccentric for this, and people do not diminish their characters accordingly, as if for a higher end—on the contrary, it calls for rather greater intelligence and interest in daily affairs: the cowshed and the kitchen become as vital as the abstractions of love or friendship. But the chart is naturally affected by private disturbances, and so everyone is on the lookout. The chief question of the day begins, 'Where is?' for there is a place and a purpose and a surveillance for everyone. In the absence of any sanctions it has to be so—anarchy tempered by a watch-committee of the whole community is total government.

It therefore became immediately obvious that Dieter was seeking me out in order to have private conversations. 'Where is Dieter?' bred suspicion. My friends on the kibbutz were politely inquisitive, sniffing the air for an odour of decay that might threaten gangrene. Conspiracy is the opposite of gossip. I could not reveal Dieter's distress beyond vague mentions that it was all rather hard for him here—something which they were all the more anxious to alleviate—and so I fell back on the excuse that he had naturally gravitated towards me as the only other foreigner with whom he could speak German. When the air is full of such unspoken questioning, as powerful as sound waves, it is hard to stay unreceptive, and Dieter sensed that his weakness had been found out, so that he tried to cover up in the hours of work by drawing as close as he could to his friends in the *Nahal*. One afternoon they played a game in the swimming pool which consisted of keeping a permanent chain of divers in rotation. No sooner had a man jumped off the diving board than another took his place, and a third and fourth were already climbing up the iron ladder. Arms and legs and breathless bodies beating the water formed a moving circle, and Dieter fitted himself into this procession, his serious face never relaxing for a moment although all the others were yelling and throwing themselves in and showing off. Finally they all gave up after a free-for-all ducking competition. The tension eased up after this, for it seemed that Dieter was having a good time after all.

Soon afterwards an English couple turned up. The summer tourist round was beginning, the new Grand Tour of students and layabouts and rolling-stones, passing from one kibbutz to the next in search of free board and food, the minimum of work and 'experience'. The word has swept round the Mediterranean that the kibbutz is a good thing, and in full summer, most kibbutzim are swamped by these locusts, for it requires a fine balance to get any good work out of them, and yet avoid the charge of authoritarianism which these migrants are prone to throw around. With an intuitive knack, the English couple singled us out at supper as the two most useful foreigners and joined the table where we were sitting. It was uncomfortable to receive the reactions coming from the surrounding tables: nothing easy to define, nothing ostensible but merely the sense of a new regrouping. The couple were both tall, rather strikingly handsome, although on second inspection these good looks seemed to derive from their self-confident manner. Almost immediately they began to complain—the wife wanted something different to eat because her stomach had been upset at the last kibbutz, and they were about to apply to the secretary for a larger room because they could not fit into the accommodation offered to them in their present hut. I tried to dissociate myself from their conspicuous behaviour, and at the same time to warn them that it would not be welcome, and they should be prepared to move on soon. Naturally they took this for granted.

The next day neither of them turned up for work. It did not seem a coincidence that Dieter and I were paired together all morning, although this had never happened before. At breakfast, too, the husband was being rude in the kitchen, shouting that his wife was to have breakfast in bed because she was ill. 'Doesn't anybody here understand English?' The placid cooks understood clearly. One becomes self-conscious abroad about one's countrymen. The sins and failures of the English—so indignantly attacked at home—are now one's property none the less. I realized that it was going to be them or me, and the only concern was not to drag Dieter into a clash of values which would be incomprehensible to him. My friends at the kibbutz withdrew from the contest: they were too polite to argue or take much notice. Strangers are after all strangers.

The moment of conflict came unexpectedly one morning. The husband had been unable to dodge any more work, although he disputed the work-sheet pinned up on the notice-board every evening to announce the following day's programme. He claimed to be a qualified electrician, and so agricultural labour was a waste of his skill. On his second day he deliberately missed the lorry leaving at 4 o'clock. As Yitzhak, the dark-skinned Iraqi, swung on to the back with his usual sleepiness at the gates, the husband was seen waving in the distance, but he was deliberately ignored. Later he was made to understand that he was not to repeat this kind of thing if he intended staying, and he had since been punctual. When the first flush of the dawn had gone, and the heat began to oppress, he would grow bored and pay no attention to what he was doing. Walking behind the trees in the orchard on this occasion, he came up to me and asked me what I was doing on a kibbutz. Picking a peach, he sat down under the trees and skinned it, carefully catching the drops of juice with his tongue. Then he lay back to enjoy the peach. I was silly enough to stop picking and walk round the tree to where I could watch him, and where we were concealed from the others. When he had finished, he lit a cigarette, and then launched into an attack on the way a kibbutz tried to resemble a kindergarten. I was about to answer him when the branches were swept aside and Gingi came through. He was the supervisor appointed for the morning, a young man of twenty-four with a thatch of red hair which gave him his nickname and the burnt-brick complexion which someone of his colouring acquires under strong sun. Very mildly he asked us to do what was required of us. I scooted off, ashamed to listen to the argument that then took place under the tree.

Naturally Gingi gave an account of this incident: it almost seemed to precede us home, flashing as if by heliograph through the empty landscape. In such circumstances, the trim kibbutz becomes oppressive. Self-justification needs to be evident, not audible, to people who have put so much at stake. Honesty at work is furthermore the chief criterion—the work need not be good because a movement back to the land demands rigorous training, but it must be whole-hearted. Once I heard an old *kibbutznik* say that the only test of a good kibbutz was to see how many men turned up after a hard day's work and after they had washed and changed, to help unload a lorry-load of beet which arrived unexpectedly just before the evening meal. In a good kibbutz, all the men should be prepared to help. This is the only way to appreciate the service to the community, for romantic notions of dedication to an ideal tend to wither under the repetitions and fatigues of a hard life. The lawns and gardens, so carefully watered, the smiling little houses, like playthings with their pink tiled roofs and square matchbox corners and regularity, becomes a reproach. The community's purpose, its existence, is wholly utilitarian: only its justification is utopian. Guilt and mental or physical parasitism are insupportable. Insufficiency or self-doubt can be converted to use, for a skilful application to the right work can release energy from these worries. Once I had perceived this, it was time for me to move on. Others could take the experience of sharing life vicariously. Plumbing my own insufficiency on this score, I did not wish to witness the inevitable failure of the English couple, and prepared to concede their temporary but prior victory over me.

I told Dieter as much. He had already heard of the morning's episode, so ramified is the system of gossip. Someone had told the Italian boy, and he had come to tell Dieter. As a matter of fact, Gingi was rather a friend of his, and had come to say that I was not to take it to heart, that he had seen whose fault it was. It was little consolation, for I had already been rebuked, in the kindest possible way, by the mere knowledge which my friends had acquired. Even Israel looked somewhat put out—or so I imagined—when I asked him for the loan of his hammock to have my siesta. In the evening, I made it clear that my time was running short, that I would have to leave the kibbutz in the next few days. The news created another tiny regrouping, as some thought I was being frivolous, some held that it was high time, and others that I was making a mistake. The breach became all the more noticeable in that the wife marked her complete recovery of health by appearing in a pair of purple slacks with a shirt to match and very heavy make-up. Make-up on a kibbutz is still a rarity, and rather frowned on, not for simple Puritanical motives but because it accentuates the value of a woman in respects which are not considered essential. In the evening she went to the children's house, to help put them to bed, and created such a furore that it took half an hour longer than usual to calm the dormitories. The couple were making the most of their victory.

Dieter was upset. We talked over plans, and in order to console him and provide a change of atmosphere, I decided that we would make a farewell expedition. The Dead Sea scenery is majestic but Dieter had been too busy to visit it while he was working at Dimona. He was doubtful now, searching for the levity of my intentions. But I persuaded him that he should see the fortress of Massada, massive above the Dead Sea, memorable for its heroic defence against the Romans, at whose conclusion its nine hundred guerillas took their own lives sooner than fall into the hands of the legionaries. The story inevitably appealed to Dieter who took it as highly symbolic of the Jewish condition, and relevant to the contemporary state of Israel. Going to the secretary of the kibbutz, we asked if we might take off the following day for the expedition. Dieter would later have to make up for the missing hours by voluntary work during his leisure: I was already outside the fold. Permission was given, largely because the schoolchildren were to make an educational tour of the fortress later in the month, and Massada was therefore a subject of topical interest.

My car had been left in the road outside the kibbutz. A trough grimy with cattle dip against foot and mouth, and into which all humans had to lower their shoes and sandals, lay sunken across the road. On abandoning the car outside the gates in this way, a *kibbutznik* friend had advised me to lock it as a precaution. As the nearest habitation was the aerodrome about ten miles away, and the kibbutz was at the very end of a road which led only up to it, I had asked him if he did not trust the members of a community who had come together specifically to renounce property. The car had remained locked, however, as if I were clinging to my possession whatever my life inside the kibbutz might be. Now at a quarter to four, as the others were being woken for work, Dieter and I slipped through the trees across the dewy grass and across Israel's careful gardens to the car. The sky was still a velvet grey, cold enough for us to shiver.

The road to Sodom and on to Massada lies like a strip of grey matting over the open desert. It makes the sandy desolation which recedes into the distance even more sinister and frightening. It is only possible to live with the desert-waste on its own terms like the Bedouin. The slow encroachment is implacable. So the fine sand drifting on to the new tarmac is a warning, and as one clings in that open aridity to the thin stretch of human endeavour, relying on the incessant hum of the engine, it is easy to suffer from the frailty of one's position, and to fear the ultimate fate of engulfment. For miles along the road there are no signs of life, unless perhaps a conduit or an incongruous, prefabricated bridge, stranded as if in ruins. Outside Beersheba, and occasionally visible further out in the desert, are the clustered Bedouin settlements of low-pitched black tents, riding the tide of the sands. The sight of a camel is more of a reassurance and guarantee of survival than any petrol engine. Gradually the landscape is transformed, as the sand imperceptibly gives way to crumbling sand-rock, baked but flaking throughout the years, and finally to rock itself. With a sudden transition, a cleft opens up below, rifting the plateau like a deep, long gash. In the distance the Dead Sea shimmers its artificial peroxide welcome, like a swimming pool on a hot day which suddenly proves bitter and tepid with chlorine. At the most dramatic viewpoint, where the reddish rocks stretch for miles, scratching the Jordan skyline, the road hairpins down to Sodom, already sultry at seven o'clock in the morning. The potash works add another feature of unreality to the surroundings, and another smell to the air, strong with chemicals. A few small huts, thrown like litter around the shore of the lake, form the nucleus of the town. The earth has been beaten down into an ochre or black loess, and the tarmac gives out short of Sodom, although a new road is being built, slowly and listlessly through the summer heat. All round lies the desolation of an abandoned outpost—in the broken hulks of lorries, the scrap machinery, the rusty narrow-gauge railway—and it gives the impression that the expenditure of energy only adds to the sullenness of the atmosphere. Rotting boats are moored along the edge of the lake, stuck fast, almost petrified into the solid salt which fringes the water. Shutters hang off the windows of the huts, the slats unhinged and unpainted. It is a location for the dry and the sere, for those whose blood is no longer fresh but has thickened to a yellow bile, sedentary enough to enable them to survive.

By the time we reached Massada, it was already seven o'clock and the sun was orange in the sky. Laboriously Dieter and I set out up the Serpent, as the pathway ramp up to the fortress is called by Flavius Josephus, the historian of the war with the Romans. It was nine before we reached the top, dizzy with the effort. Down below were clearly visible the foundations of the besieging Roman camp. Dieter was silent, except when he went off on short forays to estimate the cubic capacity of the cistern or to discover where the granary could have been. Since he refused to wear a hat, the bridge of his nose blazed a vivid crimson, and in his khaki shorts, he was every centimetre the German tourist. When at last we climbed down to the foot of the mountain I drove on round the Dead Sea over the flinty track towards Ein Gedi where a frontier kibbutz has been established. The houses there have cooling systems installed, which makes the heat supportable, and there is a waterfall dropping from a mountain spring into a natural pool. Pushing through bamboo thickets and a luxuriance of tropical plants, we made our way to this pool, trapped among rocks and boulders. The ice-cold waterfalls splashing down a smooth face and with relief we lay along the stone. It was after this shower that Dieter told me what he had decided: that he was going to stay in Israel for the rest of his life. Talk for him was not a dialogue, but a process of un-burdening, and there was nothing I could say, as we stretched out on our backs in the shallows with only our heads above water and the fall cascading behind us. When he had finished, I told him that he was transferring the parable of Sodom and Gomorrah to modern times; that the Dead Sea valley is a place for atonement; but plainly his decision was the result of long brooding, and nothing from me would reverse it. Some state of exaltation had mastered him, as it can do with solitary men, the hermits within the world. Fortunately another bather, an American in sleek cotton shorts, came up the path, and put an end to Dieter's monologue of self-justification. The man started to tell us how pleasant the climate here was after last summer in Bangkok, and even Dieter appreciated that it was time to leave.

Stopping at the kibbutz, we wandered around in the garden, among the tamarisk trees and the burnt lawns and the cages for tame peacocks and guineafowl. Although it was still not the full sun of midsummer, it was torrid enough to induce a complete lassitude. Below us, not far from the shores of the lake, the members of the kibbutz were out at work lifting stones by hand off a dug field. A high wall showed how much they had already achieved. I lay down under the shade of a hut, and within reach of a tap, while Dieter in his mood of excitement went down the hill to volunteer for stone-lifting.

He earned us our lunch. We sat with some thirty sweat-stained men in a decrepit dining-hut, alive with flies and wasps and huge golden-bodied hornets. There was almost no talk as we cut up our salads of tomato and cucumber. If somebody wanted something, he got up and fetched it. The mode of life was eremitical: each man was incapsulated in himself because an outward display could only tax his already strained colleagues. The kibbutz might almost have been under a self-imposed vow of monasticism. Nobody made any reference to Dieter's voluntary work although he had been the only man in the fields who was not permanently living in this kibbutz. It was all that Dieter longed for, a kind of Foreign Legion camaraderie. Out of the corner of his eyes he was observing all their gestures, apeing their roughness.

On the way home, as we veered slowly over the sharp flints of the track hugging the Dead Sea shore, he explained at greater length how this was the only life for him, and how necessary it was for him to make amends, to come to terms with the Jews, especially the Israelis—he was going to apply for permission to stay on our kibbutz. In order not to be late returning, we stopped for only a few minutes at the single café in Sodom, the *Lot's Wife*, to have the drink one needs every half-hour in that climate. A Franciscan monk was collecting lumps of solid salt from the cliff behind the café, and presenting them to his coachload of extenuated tourists. In the gathering dusk the road back was nothing like so isolating and agoraphobic. Nights shrink the desert. We stopped at Dimona for Dieter to show me the houses which he and his group had built and again in Beersheba for an ice at a shop which has a reputation throughout the Negev for its water-ices. At one of the little tables were sitting the English couple, who immediately invited us to join them. It became obvious that they had been drinking earlier. The husband explained how they had thumbed a lift in from the kibbutz because they couldn't stand the boredom of it any longer. It offended him that we had gone off to the Dead Sea without him. 'And I never knew you had a car,' he complained. 'GB. The old Gor-Blimey plates, you brought it all the way from home?' He tried to persuade us to return to the bar which they had just left—and to bring the Kraut along, as he referred to Dieter. To his disgust we left them to go alone; they even spurned the offer of a free ride back.

When we reached the kibbutz, Dieter went off to find the secretary. I did my packing, throwing the few clothes I had into my knapsack, and then walked to the children's house to find my friends who were putting their daughter to bed. It was after supper that Israel came to have a word with me, modestly inviting me to walk with him round the strip of concrete which ringed the kibbutz, irregularly leading from hut to hut. It took us quite soon to Israel's patch of garden, which he had reduced almost to mud with heavy watering, and now almost automatically he started to fiddle about with some shrubs. When he came to the point, it was to say that

he had been sent for by the secretary and informed of
Dieter's request to stay on the kibbutz for a year. The
secretary knew all about Dieter because Israel had been
relaying the conversations which he had overheard through
the thin walls, and there could be no question of Dieter
staying on the kibbutz—for his sake as much as theirs.
Other people might feel differently, he said, but to them
Dieter appeared a sick man, and therefore they had decided
that as I had some influence on him, I should drive him
away in the morning, when I left. It was important that I
should explain to Dieter the reasons why he should not stay:
that would be less painful than an abrupt refusal from the
secretary.

Dieter accepted the verdict with great composure, and it
never crossed his mind to appeal. In the erratic course of
his emotions lay the evidence of his sickness perhaps, or
maybe it was relief that someone had taken a firm decision
for him. He was very tired after the heavy day's work and
heat, and only wanted to go to sleep. I told Israel that we
would be off in the morning.

So we found ourselves putting our luggage into my car
shortly after dawn, in the clear still light which showed all
the details of the kibbutz in such relief—the solid dining-
hall, the distant swimming pool, the water tower, the cattle
sheds. Only Israel came slipping through the little outwork
of trees to see us off. He had a request to make. It seemed
that during the night the English couple had telephoned the
kibbutz incessantly, announcing that they were stranded in
Beersheba with no means of getting home and they wanted
transport from the kibbutz to fetch them. Furthermore, it
was plain that they were offensively drunk, shouting down
the line, until finally they were too drunk to telephone. The
secretary had told them that they were no concern of his,
and he advised them to spend the night in Beersheba. In the
end they had finished up in the youth hostel, only to be
turned out because they were still drinking. In the early
hours of the morning they had arrived at the kibbutz in the

local taxi which they had refused to pay, until the driver woke up the secretary, who had paid and ordered the couple to behave themselves, whereupon they had insulted and sworn at him.

While Israel was recounting all this, the couple walked up and got into the car. They had overheard the last part of the story, but perhaps spoke no French, for they said nothing. In the shed opposite us, the cows were being milked, and were lowing. The lorry had taken the workers off to the fields—everyone was at work except this little group at the car. It was like being expelled from school. Israel's young-old face held on to its usual mixture of expressions, something like the headmaster's poise between mockery or relief, melancholy or amusement. The wrinkles on his face bore no relation to the passing years, but were like linen folds, taking lines of their own. His blue overalls had been washed to a canvas grey. As I drove down the road, I saw the men at work some distance away in the fields, little black dots like pegs holding the green fields in place on the yellow background. One could almost feel the uplift that they would all experience at getting rid of this ugly foreign invasion. Silent in the back, the English couple had a certain solemnity, even though it was just the stupor of a hangover which they had had only about three hours to sleep off. In Beersheba it was the weekly market-day and they wanted to be dropped there. The streets were full of black-robed and veiled Bedouin women, their families squatting on the pavements, their men leading camels. The husband said that it had been their intention to stay up all night to see this market but they had needed to distract themselves because the kibbutz had bored them so intensely. His ambition was to join the Bedouin and live with them for a bit, and he was not worried to hear that he would need a permit from the military government. 'I'm fond of nomads,' he said, 'I'm a bit of one myself.' They got out at the main crossroads of the town, and stood on the corner, watched by some incredulous Bedouin boys. I asked him where he would go. 'Right now I'm off to Dimona,' he replied. 'There's a labour shortage there and they can do with an electrician like me. My wife's a typist so she can always get a job. It's useful, especially if I want to go off and live with the Bedouin.' They made off into the crowd, long-legged and tall, strikingly upright in the pitiful, crouching, shrouded crowd around them.

Dieter and I turned north to Tel Aviv.

II

Stands were up along the streets of Tel Aviv. Bunting and blue-and-white Israeli flags and banners flew like swallows. In the outskirts of the city, temporary bivouacs dotted the open spaces where the soldiers were quartered for the parade. Tanks and armoured cars were drawn up, being cleaned and polished for the Independence Day celebrations. Neither Dieter nor I knew that these were to have taken place, and the discovery compensated him for some of the depression which had settled on him. Finding myself responsible for Dieter in this way, I was at a loss. We had nowhere to spend the night in Tel Aviv and plainly nothing was going to make Dieter leave before tomorrow's cele-brations. There was therefore no question of driving to my flat in Haifa, but it was impossible in any case to inflict Dieter on friends like Ada, while the Ruppin Street flat was now occupied by its rightful owners. Manoeuvring Dieter out of earshot into a café, I telephoned Zvi, an Oxford friend of mine, and explained the situation to him. Once a serious student, Zvi was now a serious banker, and in some ways an Israeli counterpart to Dieter, taking himself and his ambitions quite uncritically. Being a successful young executive, he lived in a comfortable and large flat in Dubnoff Street. Methodically he assembled the facts about Dieter, and decided on the evidence that we could spend the night in his spare-room, on the condition that he did not have to accompany us to the parade.

In the evening when they met, they were uneasy in each

other's company. To Zvi the parade was one of those national lapses into chauvinism which could only be excused by the country's youth. Dieter saw it as the necessary expression of the right to exist. They argued for a while, and later Zvi took me aside to ask me if I remembered who had made a speech about the relative merits of guns and butter.

For the parade we were out early in the streets, joining the streams of spectators. To them, this was one of the sights of the year, a public entertainment: for Dieter, however, it was the embodiment of Israel militant, the new force which had arisen to take charge of the Jewish destiny. I could see all Dieter's suppressed hysteria again rising to the surface, breaking through the serious clamps which he had imposed upon himself. Anything which represented a defiance of his hated, inviolate past was a symbol of the great gestures of human independence: the Israeli armed forces fitted perfectly into the symbolic framework. In the easy-going, good-natured crowd, Dieter's face stood out, conspicuous for its intensity verging on fanaticism. Arriving much too early, we secured a place right down on the pavement from where we would be able to see the parade moving towards us from the far distance. Further along, the stands slowly filled up, and behind us the crowd thickened. A rope separated us from the street and soldiers took up their positions in front, lining the route. Immediately before us lounged a young officer with a transistor wireless playing light music. Dieter was slightly shocked by his negligence and the holiday spirit of those around us who were eating and laughing and paying no attention. When the march past began, however, it was no disappointment to him. Aeroplanes screamed overhead, probably the same jet fighter-bombers which had broken the morning stillness over our cotton crops at the kibbutz. Then detachments of the army and navy, both men and women, swung purposely past, their rubber boots thumping the tarmac with hard truncheon-beats. A man in the crowd, mistaking Dieter's nationality, explained to him in broken English to which branch of the forces each squad belonged. Then, with a roar which made the pavement under us tremble, rumbled the heavy equipment, the armour and the artillery. I could see that Dieter was transfixed. Later as we walked away, he began to exult about the fight which this army could put up. Not wishing to argue with him about politics, I arranged to meet him in the evening in Zvi's flat. As it turned out, Dieter spent most of the day in a transit camp at Jaffa, talking to the soldiers and clambering about inside the tanks.

After dark we took to the streets once more, Zvi wryly consenting to come with us. From far off, the noise was tumultuous, and even in the flat we had been able to hear the crowd in the nearby thoroughfare of Ibn Gavirol, making its way to the centre of the town. Fireworks were being let off; everybody appeared to possess a toy trumpet fitted up with a squeaker; chains of people were going down the streets singing, their arms linked. We walked as far as Dizengoff where most people had assembled: the squeakers were constantly pushed under one's nose and then blared, so that the only retaliation was for us to buy some and then blow back. From the third-floor balcony of a café, a large blonde woman with a Hollywood bosom was singing into a microphone. Everyone joined in the choruses. There were attempts to pull her away from the balcony, as others wanted to sing, but she fought back, getting her clothes ripped. We drifted along with the crowd, blowing our paper trumpets. Across the streets, the long lines of people holding hands were now catching at passers-by and forcing them to join in.

> Three German officers crossed the Rhine,
> *Parlez-vous*!

Each chain spread the song down the street, louder and louder, yelling the unfamiliar Hebrew words of the tune. Laughing faces swept by, whipped along the street by the closely-held hands. Dieter was caught up by the end of the line, and with his usual expression of earnestness, he began to join in the tune. It was too much for Zvi, who had stood aside as the others came past, and he ran after Dieter and pulled him away. I was glad that I was left behind and unable to catch up through the press for some time. Turning against the moving mass in the streets, we elbowed our way home. The oncoming crowds had started a second tune: 'Colonel Bogey'. Once more Dieter was swirled away, and this time, Zvi shrugged his shoulders. On the way home, he said that it was imperative for Dieter to leave the country, if some disaster were to be avoided. He explained himself: 'The things he admires in Israel are the things he wants to admire in his own country but can't bring himself to, not after its recent past. That's why he loves the militarism of parading and following the tanks. It's *Kamaradschaft* that he's after at a kibbutz, group spirit and communal enjoyment, the knowledge of belonging to one big, strong family. It's the emotional basis for all totalitarianism. Because the Jews have managed to survive, this man has managed to transfer his ideas of virtue to them. This kind of philo-Semite is first cousin to the anti-Semite.'

Zvi tried to explain this again to Dieter the following morning, but I would not stay and listen. Dieter seemed to take it to heart—he could understand an outburst of this sort—and afterwards he was prepared to drive with me to Haifa, down the streets still decorated with bunting, the litter thick on the ground, and the bare planks and scaffolding of the empty stands looking gaunt along the road. It hardly mattered which ship Dieter took now—he was too confused to plan much, and discussion of his problem was closed as far as I was concerned. Recrimination was out of the question, and Dieter would have to reflect about it all by himself. He sat about quietly in my flat, going down to the Carmel beach to bathe in the afternoons.

On a morning of brilliant clarity, I took him down to the harbour. Across the bay, the town of Acre stood out clearly on its promontory, the customary haze having evaporated. Nothing could have been more peaceful when we set off from the top of the Carmel—the empty sky and the flat sea, the ordered city with its ships moored in the docks like toys in the distance. Inside the port area, too, there was the regular calm of organized work. After the formalities, I went on board with Dieter, who was travelling deck-class, and we made our way to the stern through a maze of ironwork ladders and restricted decks. It was important to stake out the best floorspace on the deck, away from the smoke-stack, and as protected as possible from the wind. With his sleeping-bag and windjammer, he would be quite comfortable, and I had given him a provision of food. The liner stopped along the route, which would give him chance to restock. Laying it out on the scrubbed planks, we established the claim for his sleeping-bag. Other tourist passengers were milling around, young men with beards, tough girls in shorts, the independent Bohemian flotsam which goes rolling round the world in the summer—Australians and Americans, a negro or two, an artist, an English student. By one of those coincidences so frequent in this life of ports and hitch-hikes and cheap travel, I met an English girl whom I had briefly known on the kibbutz, and I introduced her to Dieter, whom she would have to tolerate at close quarters for the full five days to Venice. The three of us explored the boat, the single tourist lavatory, the second-class deck-chairs behind padlocked railings, the forbidden first-class swimming pool. There were three hours before the boat sailed. I said good-bye to Dieter, taking with me the final image of that earnest ugly, puzzled, red-burnt face. The girl leaned over the taffrail and waved. She was going up to the university to read mathematics, I could remember, and she had been rather popular at the kibbutz, for she had known how to iron shirts properly, and had some previous experience of farming.

III

By chance, I went back to the kibbutz: I had not intended to return but a couple there who had come back from a honeymoon in Europe invited me to call on them. The season had changed when I returned. It was cold at nights now, and by day there was even some rain. Mud was the last thing to expect in the Negev. If the daylight was still uniquely blue, it had a brittle quality, as if it might splinter like a pane of glass.

On this occasion I was not staying in my old hut in the Vatican, but in a modern bungalow where my friends were living. It was at a weekend and it was somehow assumed that my visit was a social, and not a functional, occasion, so incongruously in this workaday atmosphere I sat about and lazed. Perhaps Israel deliberately avoided me: for three days I never saw him. On the other hand, having established his privacy, he was able to go to ground in this way. It would have been unthinkable for anyone else to remain so concealed. Eventually I went along to his room and knocked at the door. He came sidling out, and shut the door quickly behind him, so that even on this occasion I never entered his room. We stepped outside. He was as usual in his blue overalls, looking particularly infantile with his soft face and tidy hair. Finding no words, I merely showed him the letter which I had received from Dieter some weeks before:

I'm sorry you had me on your hands like that, because I was such a nuisance to everybody, it seems. When I came to Israel, I was full of hope for a new life for myself. No doubt my emotions were foolish for I was certainly trying to atone for the guilt of others in order to be free myself. The Jews were destroyed by my country and Israel is the unwitting result. I came to Israel and was destroyed in turn. Do not compare my little disaster please, that would be too ironic. What I mean is that now I shall never get this Jewish thing—whatever it is—into a perspective that I can live with. But perhaps I never would have done anyhow.

The letter went on to describe his journey, and I tried to read into its lighter tone an affair with the girl. At least,

Dieter was back at his studies and presumably behaving in a more conventional way. Israel was unimpressed: he shrugged. 'Very sad. It's a pity that we should alienate our friends by just being in this country. But what do you want? *que voulez-vous*? You see, we were right to get him to leave.' I agreed with him.

'How should we be responsible for what other people think of us? We are getting on with our lives. *On continue*. There are priorities, and survival comes top.' We walked round his garden for a bit, while he picked the heads off some dead roses. 'That's all that is left for us of this Jewish thing.'

'What happened to that English couple who were also here at the time?' I asked at length.

'Oh them,' he laughed. 'They're still in Dimona, or they were when I last heard. He's the electrician there, and they say there's a big sale in candles.'

Chapter Eight

ZVI

PURIM: CARNIVAL TIME, FANCY dress masquerades, an
excuse for national gaiety, for it is almost the only cheerful
Jewish holiday in the year, bright among the festivals of
lamentations. There is an almost legendary story of a Purim
party in Tel Aviv one year to which a young man went
disguised in ultra-orthodox clothes. When he was leaving
the party about three in the morning, he walked over to his
sports car and began to lower the hood, in order to drive
home in the cool air of the coming dawn. He was still in his
fancy dress, and a policeman came hurrying over the square
on the grounds that any orthodox Jew caught tampering
with a car during a high holiday must be intending some
damage. It was suspicious that a student from B'nai Brak,
the religious district on the outskirts of Tel Aviv, should
claim to possess an Alfa-Romeo, but when the young man
asked the policeman to pull his side-curls and prove that
they would come off, there was every excuse for arrest.
Assault of that kind would make a bad impression in court.
In the police station the young man stripped and then was
obliged to walk through the streets back to his car with his
hired clothes under his arm.

Zvi—who told me this story—was the kind of man to
think such a practical joke funny. It lay somehow within the
bounds of what was permissible, while poking fun at these
limits; covering a basic conservatism with an appearance of
cynicism. Zvi's grandfather had come to Israel after the

Russian pogroms at the beginning of the century, bringing enough money with him to buy an orange grove. This was exceptional; and if such a thing as a gentleman farmer could exist in Israel, it would have been Zvi, for he had that kind of arrogance, or self-confidence. In fact he was a banker because for some time past the oranges could be more profitably converted into bungalows. But an uncle of his still lived in the large mouldering house in Rehovoth, where he could supervise the remaining orchards. There was a decayed Edwardian atmosphere about the place, with its pillared gateway and short drive decorated with cracked vases, its peeling stucco and family photographs all over the cavernous rooms. Although he had been brought up in this house, Zvi preferred to live in Tel Aviv, and only rarely visited his property, and then rather as a Chekovian land-owner. When he was eighteen, he had been sent to England and once he was there, he had won a scholarship to Oxford. Three years at the university had provided the intellectual superstructure which a temperament like his required. He knew that he was going to make a lot of money, and he knew that there were a lot of underprivileged people who weren't going to. He also saw what happened in between the two ends of this scale: an Oxford education, in short, had imbued him with its most insidious characteristic, a genuine appreciative snobbery. Zvi took pleasure in his white settler attitudes, quite aware that they were attitudes, and would tell acquaintances about his family and their early coloni-zation in the old days of Turkish rule, and how his grand-father had enlisted in the Turkish army in the first world war, only to desert after the Balfour Declaration. He would explain that those immigrants who had come to Israel then were either cranky Zionists or else the scum of European Jewry, for anybody with sense or money or enterprise would rightly have preferred America. It was the same with recent immigration, he would go on, the wealthy, the middle classes or the skilled workers went to make their lives in Europe or the New World, depending on which

country they had just left. The others, the debilitated and
the old, came to Israel really only to die in the unexpected
atmosphere of a Jewish welfare state run for their benefit.
Israel had always depended on outside contributions to
keep afloat the uneconomic proposition of its existence—a
tradition dating back to the days when pious Jews were
subsidized to live out their last years in the Holy Land and
also from the turn of this century when the Jews who were
making good in America would send over dollars to their
less fortunate brethren who had failed to follow the rush to
the west. Once again, though, his three years at Oxford had
taught him when to stop short of his conclusions, and with
a charming smile he would acknowledge that it was impossible to have a traditionalist or free-opportunity society in
the circumstances in which he had grown up. There just
would be no state of Israel.

Zvi lived comfortably, even prosperously, set apart a
little from the life round him by his American car, his up-
to-the-minute books, his capitalist friends and outlook.
Living in a luxury flat in Dubnoff Street in the centre of
Tel Aviv, he settled into a life that was something of a
phenomenon in this society. It was impossible to decide
whether he played golf at Caesarea at the weekends because
he enjoyed it or because he felt that it was incumbent on
him, with his memory of young men roaring off in their
sports cars across Magdalen Bridge for an afternoon at
Huntercombe. He saw his circle of friends, however, like-
minded bankers and stockbrokers, the foreign diplomats
and the civil servants. They wore suits and ties and wouldn't
have dined out in the summer in an open-necked shirt,
although the convention allowed the tie to be taken off in
very humid weather. Zvi liked a certain formality: he had
regularly attended dining-clubs at Oxford. It was all the
more surprising, therefore, to find him at this particular
fancy dress party, for the other people were altogether more
carefree and Bohemian than he, but perhaps this corresponded to the man-of-the-world side of his character. Most

people there had made some effort with their clothes, patching up a disguise of some sort, but Zvi remained true to himself in a dark blue suit.

The party was given on the ground floor of the house, with long French windows giving on to a terrace and to a small garden beyond. We sat about on chairs or on the ground eating the buffet supper. Other people arrived until the room became crowded, a gramophone was turned on and as the meal ended, slowly the dancing began. The party took some time to get under way, but there was a great deal to drink and the food had been excellent, and as others arrived, the carnival mood built up. It was planned that the whole party would move on later anyhow, as there were things to do and see in the streets, and talk of an open-air band. When the records came to an end, and the couples dancing in the room broke up, a girl stepped forward and started to sing. She was an actress from the Habimah theatre; her songs came from some folk opera. The rhythms invited the guests to clap hands, to stamp their feet or join in the chorus, and soon most of the people in the room were accompanying her. The atmosphere had been set up for a kind of cabaret, so that by the time she finished singing the audience were looking round for something else. There was an attempt to sing another song, with a few hearty people rousing the others. In the aftermath Zvi stepped forward, almost as if he had been billed for the next number. He had borrowed a large black trilby from somewhere, but it was too big for him and rested on his ears, making him look ludicrous. Although he was strongly-built and healthy-looking, now he seemed scrawny and top-heavy as if moving on stunted legs. First of all he made a little speech in a mock Yiddish accent about the rising cost of living, the difficulty of making ends meet, his enormous family of starving children. Then with great speed and agility, he skipped round the room, darting from person to person, pretending to examine their jewellery and then offering to exchange it or to buy it. He would haggle over prices, taking both sides of the bargain. Through his bartering too, he was keeping up a quick-fire account of his daily life, of his business, of the hard times and the iniquity of the Russian officials. Zvi was speaking a guttural Hebrew with snatches of improvised Yiddish, which he certainly could not speak properly. All the time the hat kept falling off or slipping down on to his forehead and he would rapidly push it back into place. Going up to the women, he fingered their necklaces, bracelets or watches and tried to persuade their owners to give him these jewels until he had his hands full and a few long strings of beads were also hanging out of his pockets. Then he sat cross-legged on the floor, and with clawing, rapid little gestures began to arrange this collection, to sort the jewels out, evaluate them and inspect them, accompanying the patter with the shifty looks of a stage villain. It was a horrifying, almost obscene, caricature of the shabby Jewish trader, and through his talk, we could understand that Zvi was impersonating the Jewish pawnbroker of a hundred years ago in Odessa, where his family had come from originally. Everybody was shrieking with laughter and joining in the imitation. Some snatched at the jewels on the floor and Zvi rolled about to clutch at them, moaning that he was being robbed, while others shouted that they wanted to buy something and started to argue over the price. Hardly anybody seemed offended—behind me there was a huge man asking why in the folk-lore on this subject, the Jewish trader was always assumed to be so *small*, a poor little Jew. Finally Zvi brought the joke to an end, sweeping up all the objects from the floor and then going round the room to hand them back, still haggling and disparaging their value though, complaining now in a normal voice that he would be ruined, that it was all a trick to send him to prison. At last he took off the awful hat, and a few minutes later, the cabaret was over, the little jeweller from Odessa had disappeared to wash his hands and comb his hair and Zvi the handsome Israeli with the detached Oxford manner was once more in his place. Everybody crowded round to congratulate him on his party piece; it had been as good as a play, a wonderful bit of acting, the funniest slapstick. Where had he learnt it all from? He was teased that this was how he had started his career as a banker, that now they knew the origins of his money. The gramophone was turned on again, and couples started to twist. Coffee was made and more drink produced: the party continued until it was time to move on, to join in the larger carnival of the city. Then the guests pushed down the narrow passage to the front door, and set off to merge into the noise of the streets, into the crowds of men and women parading their cheerfulness. Only Zvi, sombre in his dark suit and with his quizzical expression, struck a dissonant note as he stood for a moment on the pavement and then, walking to his car, drove away into the covering night.

Chapter Nine

EAST AND WEST

I

I MET HIM ONLY with other people—we had friends in common who were also neighbours of mine for a brief period, so that I used to drop in for a cup of coffee or a drink, and on three or four occasions this man was there. His appearance was somehow emphatic, so that he appeared to dominate the room although he was generally modest and preferred to sit back in a chair rather than push himself into the centre of the room. Perhaps it was just his large head which attracted attention, for its intelligent modelling was accentuated by his premature baldness, with the result that his forehead and the top of his skull shone as if a spotlight were focussed on to them. Everything about him spoke of neatness and efficiency, his clothes, his smile, the way he shook hands. The first opinions I heard him pronounce were on the details of a scheme to resettle the Arab refugees. He held that there were affinities between Jews and Arabs which would enable Israel to integrate into the Middle East, and with regard to such common ties and history, he called himself a Canaanite. Israel's defensive hostility towards her neighbours would have to be broken down and, as a preliminary, compensation would have to be paid to those refugees who did not want to return, while readmitting to the country those who did and rehabilitating them in the new scheme of things. He was explaining how this might be done through an impartial board, composed perhaps of

171

United Nations officials which would examine each case on the pre-supposition that each man had a right to return. It would take up to fifteen years to liquidate the problem, for he thought that Israel should reserve, in the interests of her economic structure, the counterbalancing right of laying down a system of priority in choosing which refugees were to be resettled. Priorities would depend on usefulness and potential, and would have the additional value of safeguarding Israeli security, for suspected troublemakers could be delayed entry for the maximum number of years. As he saw it, the long-term prospects for a settled Middle East rested upon the breaking down of what were essentially tribal differences, exaggerated by backward economic forms —typical post-colonial developments, in short. Meanwhile there would need to be further concessions, extra-territorial rights to the ports, boundary alterations and so on.

These opinions were put forward decisively, but with deference to others in the room who were *sabras*, although they mostly agreed to the sort of thing he was saying. But this man had been born in Leningrad, where he had spent most of his life, and he had come to Israel only three years ago. He was a scientist, a biologist with a graduate degree from Leningrad which had earned him a research job in Israel, and he now worked at an experimental agricultural station where he claimed that he could do better work than in Russia—something he had never expected.

He came from a poor Jewish family, and in normal circumstances he could never have received much education, unless perhaps a religious one. He and his family owed everything to the revolution, he said. His father had a job as janitor of a big modern block: his sister was a hospital nurse and hoped to obtain a diploma which would qualify her for further medical training. Almost all his life he had been aware of how much the new social order had improved his position, for his father had always given thanks in his prayers for the unexpected success and prosperity, contrasting their circumstances with what they might have endured,

and what most of his family and friends had undergone
during the war. It seemed to him a blessing to be able to
sweep the long flights of concrete stairs, to receive his wage,
and see his children so well taken care of. During their
childhood, this man and his sister had been brought up by
their father with Zionist aspirations none the less passionate
for being a little inarticulate. The redemption of the Jews
was his father's prayer. The son, then, had inherited a compound of Zionism and communism.

It was difficult to ask him to be explicit and anyhow he
preferred more general subjects of conversation—his
pastime was American fiction. It was also relatively seldom
that he interrupted his research work and so had a chance
to talk to his friends, but from this and later meetings I
pieced together his attitude that Israel was a synthesis of
these two opposing doctrines which had formed his character. He understood that the creation of the state of Israel was
inconsistent with Marxist theory, and he maintained that it
was a temporary historical phenomenon. History would
reconcile Jews and Arabs and put an end to nationalist
antagonisms which were a by-product of the struggle against
colonialism from which Jews and Arabs had suffered alike.
Yet he believed that there was also a historical impulse
which brought the Jews back to their country of origin,
and this was irreversible and irresistible. It might be sub-
jective romanticism but perhaps it corresponded to the next
historical phase in the Middle East, when the Arabs would
throw off the vestiges of their feudalism and evolve into
modern socialist countries. In this respect Israel might be
an example to them, and this was perhaps the modern his-
toric mission of the Jews. In such a scheme Israel's existence
was coherent and necessary, and he was therefore a Canaanite, for it was only this small group of intellectuals who had
the vision to foresee the common future of Jews and Arabs.
Most of the bourgeoisie meanwhile built up their hate of the
Arabs, and out of fear and contempt allocated huge sums to
national defence—a misconception which could only bring

about the open war of annihilation which they most dreaded. The manner of the foundation of the state of Israel worried him, but he saw it as an example of power politics. Naturally he would have preferred a spontaneous settling of the Jews without any demands for statehood, and he was angry that cold war politics had complicated the issue. It was typical of European decadence that, unable to solve the anti-Semitism which is a by-product of its culture, it had foisted it off on to weaker countries which happened to come within the European orbit at that moment. It was no consolation that the Russians had voted with the Americans on the partition question: everybody was his own politician in such a situation.

When he had completed his education, he said, he had been offered a job in Poland, which he had accepted. Finding himself isolated in a provincial town, the ideas which had been taking shape in his head at last matured, and he decided that it was time to emigrate to Israel. The Russian authorities would inevitably make difficulties for him, since there is a ban on emigration, and so he had fixed his journey through the Poles who had eased restrictions on emigration. In order not to prejudice his journey he had not returned to Russia, but had abandoned his father and sister. Zionism came first. In any case he believed that this was only temporary and he expected a big immigration of Russian Jews to Israel once the ban was lifted, partly because of anti-Semitism which he admitted was still persistent in spite of all the revolutionary work to stamp it out, but mainly because the historical traditions and processes of the Jews tended to a Zionist solution. He never regretted having left Russia, nor having forsaken his family, for he did not think of himself primarily as a highly-trained technician devoting himself on ideological grounds to an underdeveloped country, but as a Jew with a specifically Jewish purpose. Needless to say he was completely without religion and wished to eliminate Judaistic survivals from the modern state. As a formality, I asked him how he got along in the

Israeli communist party, which is quite active and has a handful of able members in the Knesset. He did not have much time for them, partly because his work was too important since it affected agricultural policy, and partly because of the communist party policy which fomented racial antagonism, as he saw it, by using the Arab minority as a stick to beat the Jewish majority. Disruption of the state was not his intention, he was not an anarchist but a communist. If there was a war, he would naturally fight because the safety of Israel was of paramount importance during the years when peace was still dependent on external cold war issues. So he had joined Mapam instead, and only for the time being. Each time I saw him, I tried to go over this contradictory ground with him, and he was usually ready to answer the barrage of questions, but I found it like walking over a marsh, the most solid-looking tufts of grass were the most deceptive, and he would soon grow bored with my pestering, and the expression on the high-domed, intelligent face would plainly say that his views were scientific and therefore readily comprehensible, containing no contradictions. As soon as he could, he would ask me what I thought of early Faulkner, or the New York Jewish school of novelists. Then this strange Russian would elude me in the party conversation.

II

Marvin had come to Israel on a Bnei Brith tour. He and some dozens of his friends had been conducted round the country in streamlined buses with glass-fitted roofs enabling them to get the panoramic vision. Impressed by the swirling landscape and the statistics banging in their ears—figures always rising to make these economic steeplejacks giddy with goodwill and success—they had all returned to the States, except Marvin. Essentially a belonger to groups and organizations and fraternities, a follower of any lead in fashion, social life, financial desires and politics, he had some-how managed to detach himself from the indistinguishable ruck of hearty faces, of muscular Sons of the Covenant swollen into tight T-shirts and summer pants. He wanted to know more about Israel, to transmute statistics into experience. Once one had grasped this clue, one could see in Marvin's eyes an alienated, subdued self, a man who believed that life existed somewhere apart from him, but who always went along with things because it was easier. He wanted something real. He had not yet quite killed his little doubt that all his experiences so far had been synthetic, and now he was making his stand to find out. Saying good-bye to his friends on the Bnei Brith tour had been a wrench but they had all admired him for his determination to learn more about Israel. American Jews admire the Zionism they find in others.

Naturally Marvin had turned towards authority as soon as he was left alone. The secretary of the body controlling the kibbutz movement had advised him to settle on a kibbutz where he could learn Hebrew in an *ulpan* and at the same time work to support himself, and he recommended a Mapam kibbutz which was short of labour and for which Marvin therefore volunteered. After all, it was a kind of fraternity. Nothing in his past, however, had prepared him for this. Upstate New York had provided him with a conventional Jewish bourgeois upbringing and social context. His father was permanently retained as lawyer for some Jewish business—and he also took very seriously his work as a director of a Jewish charity. As a schoolboy Marvin had belonged to Zionist organizations which had formed his image of Israel as The Old Country, and in honour of it, he had accompanied his father to the synagogue, had learnt the right songs and folk-dances, paid contributions to the funds and stuck to the Jewish boys of his own age. Pride in his home community and a sense of identity had actuated him back home, but now in Israel he felt neither, although he had been able to respond in the beginning, when he was still with his Bnei Brith tour. On the kibbutz, he seemed lost. Far from there being much sense of identity with fellow Jews, there was a bitterness of political sectionalism running through the community. Indeed, it had not been forgotten that the kibbutz had split in two on the political issue which had driven the splinter group out of Mapam. The theories and practices of communist existence had separated the extremists and moderates, dividing families and even husbands and wives, and in this kibbutz, as elsewhere in the country, the factionalists had moved to the other side of the road, installing themselves in new houses and farm buildings, taking their share of the land. As with unicellular creatures, reproduction consisted of fission. At first there had been a fence between the parent kibbutz and its offspring, and only recently had this been allowed to fall down. If the politics were beyond Marvin's emotional grasp, the traditions of the community were even more so. When faced with the fact, he could not understand that intelligent people preferred the life of peasants to any other. In particular there was a young 'cellist in the kibbutz who had given up a professional career in order to stay a farmer, and this shocked Marvin who could not accept tractor-driving as an end in itself. Once the novelty had worn off, and therefore the glamour of the exotic, Marvin came to despise himself in the banana groves where he was detailed to work, and he wanted to continue the social training which had already made it impossible for him to remain satisfied with manual labouring glorified by a cerebral ideal. It hurt Marvin to listen to the 'cellist playing at the weekends; it was a mockery of his skill, and an insult to hear the man explaining that the rough work had ruined his hands for music. The mixture of silence and gossip was both too remote and too personal for Marvin: it implied too much understanding of oneself and the others. Nor was the *ulpan* any better. Every day he would do his four hours of Hebrew, either in the classroom along with the other students, mostly Roumanians, or as preparation. It only convinced him that American was his language, and that Hebrew should be reserved for the synagogue. Nothing of the religious or Zionist fervour which had once inspired him in New York state could survive in such an atmosphere. His kind of prejudices, his kind of Jewishness, were inviolate. Self-preservation came to the front, but not before he had had several rows. Once he went to Tel Aviv and was forced to work on the Sabbath to make up for lost hours, and once or twice the intellectuals attacked him for his bourgeois morality and he could find no words to defend himself. Marvin's agony was prolonged because his father refused to answer his plea for the return fare. Perhaps he was proud of his boy doing his bit over there and wouldn't acknowledge Marvin's unhappiness. It reduced Marvin to a state of melancholy which he could not combat. At one point, he grew so worried under the pressure of abandonment that he told me why he had been to Tel Aviv—to reassure the American consul that he was not a communist. When I told him that I didn't think the authorities would be too interested that he had spent a few weeks on a kibbutz, he answered that he was afraid of losing his passport for associating with people who held such communistic ideas. He meant what he feared, which made it hard to reassure him. Fortunately his father relented and sent the vital air-ticket which brought release, the reprieve from long distance. Marvin said good-bye politely to everyone, even to the old-guard bolshevik who had led the attack on him. It was easy to see in the way that he ran out of the kibbutz how the experience would slowly change in his memory to a confusion of kindly old peasants and weird ideas and Hebrew phrases. The long grind in the lawyer's office which lay ahead would probably bring him back to Israel one day full of the complacent benevolence of upstate New York and the directorship of the Jewish charity which would fall to him in turn. Only the *kibbutzniks* would not have forgotten the mistaken American: they were now too familiar with the type.

III

The first time Achsa left Israel was with the Mapam delegation to the Moscow Youth Festival. It was hard to believe that she was doing more than taking the chance of a free ride: she had that healthy kind of prettiness which goes with ignorance of the world. The black fringe and plump cheeks and wide-smiling mouth did not add up to convictions. But she took her work in the youth movement very seriously, devoting her spare time to it, and she obviously liked parades and marches, bands and public displays. Even if social impulses and not ideology governed her actions, she was the right choice for the delegation because she was certain to make a good impression as a fresh young Israeli girl.

For a long time after her return, she was full of the excitement of it all, of the people and the places. A rival delegation from the Israeli communist party had accompanied them and she told several stories about the inevitable confusion entailed in sending two conflicting groups from so small a country to a festival like this. It was impossible to convince the ordinary spectator that the two delegations were determined not to be fused into one, not to march past together and so on. A further complication was that the young Israeli Arabs were under the communist party banner and politics with the Arab delegations were unavoidable. Still, Achsa would obviously be prepared to co-operate with anybody in such eventualities, for inside the slim athletic girl lurked a full-bosomed matron who would put order one day into innumerable classrooms. The clean white blouse and the dark gym slip would turn all too soon into a severe buttoned shirt and a full skirt: her blackboard mind would help the transformation.

The story she reported most graphically and which everyone was anxious to hear concerned an afternoon which included an event not on the programme. They were due to visit some stadium and participate in the usual sort of activity, listen to speeches or watch sports, and so they had piled into the lorry which transported them around. It was very much a part of the festival, decorated with Israeli flags, its sides blue and white with the star of David in the middle. When they drove about in this lorry, they made a habit of singing and clapping their hands in rhythm, until this noisy Mapam delegation became a distinctive part of the scene. On this occasion, they were driven a long way from the centre of Moscow but they paid little attention to the road for in the rush of the festival and the eager exhibitionistic singing which they always did, there was no time for observing the background. It did seem further away than their normal rendezvous, and when Achsa glanced out of the back of the lorry, she noticed that they were being driven through a gloomy suburb. The streets were dirty and uneven and there were none of the modern lumps of concrete which characterized the quarters of Moscow which they were shown as a rule. Suddenly the lorry stopped: it had plainly taken the wrong turning: the driver must have missed the road to the stadium. In the back they stopped singing, and pushed to the tailboard to see what was happening. Out of the side-streets came a throng of people, and Achsa described very vividly the shock she felt when she realized that these were not bystanders but a mob rushing the lorry. At first she was terrified, until with another shock she saw that they were all orthodox Jews—not the same as those she recognized from Israel, who had their dignity, but more ragged, more pitiful, and insulting to her whole sense of identity. They clutched at the lorry and shouted at the clean, pink-faced delegation, screaming for souvenirs, for something from *Eretz Israel*. Furtive fingers snatched at handbags and clothes, all their Hebrew money and coins were spirited away, blessings were yelled at them and scraps of prayers; someone was asking Achsa if she had a Torah to give them. The mob was hysterical: in no time the Israeli flags had been stripped off the lorry and had vanished.

She'd never seen anything like it, Achsa told us, and it was easy to see how offended she had been by the crude scene and its emotive power, by the Jewish tenacity which complemented but also ran counter to her Israeli personality, spreading a fundamental distaste which derived from residual fear and upsetting the facile Mapam truths which had fostered her progressive, intellectual upbringing. Achsa never discovered if the lorry-driver had taken them there on purpose but that episode swept into absurdity all the high-flying flags and brass bands and marching squads of the Moscow stadium which they eventually reached.

IV

We sat round the swimming-pool. It was a lazy day, beaten down by the heavy sky. In the hedge-enclosed garden which sheltered the pool, it was possible to feel some of the list-lessness and slack succession of the days of the Mediter-ranean Riviera, whether in France or Italy, where the idle cluster in bored, brown knots. Before us was the modern villa—sliding doors on the garden side, stone floors and glass—and from it came the steady canter of American show-biz music on the hi-fi set which no talk could swallow, no climate suppress. The grass under our wet bathing costumes was green and thin, not prickly and brown. After the splashing and submerging in the pool, we were served with a buffet lunch and the Israeli wine which starts a knocking inside the head in that summer atmosphere. Our host, Norbert was one of those Americans who devote serious attention to their diet, discussing granulated or whole-wheat bread, and looking shocked at the mention of alcohol while slopping it in too large doses into his guests' glasses.

Norbert had that cushioned expression of the rich—little pillows of good living have been pushed into awkward places to reinforce them, under the chin and around the neck and arms and stomach. He was still young enough at twenty-five to be good-looking but beyond the forceful executive it was easy to see the gross tycoon. The words and the sentiments too were still wrapped up in the language of the Harvard Business School—trends, markets and openings or opportunities. In time these too would be resolved into the flabbier simplicity of a large fortune, but for the present Norbert was still very much the graduate businessman. His transparent prolixity was the product of the school: his arguments resolved into the proposition that Israel had an excellent commercial and industrial future which he intended to exploit. It required only the operations of peace to increase this potential market throughout the Middle East. Norbert's ambition was a tiny particle of the great American dream which fitted money into all the jagged holes of the jigsaw puzzles. His wife listened attentively—the lever of it all, for she was the daughter of an industrialist, the heiress through whom the puzzles were to be solved. Her father was a self-made Israeli millionaire, no mean feat in such a country. In his way, Norbert was quite kind to his wife, Sima, ruffling her hair or kissing her in public, as much as to express his thanks. It was all part of the business—good relations with the staff.

Round the swimming pool the conversation was trivial, words dropped out between mouthfuls of salad, and anyhow stifled by the background swell of the permanent record-player. In the shiftless mood of the early afternoon, Norbert began to lecture quite formally about the country's indus-trial potential. Figures came easily to him, and plausibly, smoothed in between rhetorical questions about the per-centage of the population to own a refrigerator or who could afford higher education. A careerist after money, he would never be able to understand how solitary his obses-sion was, nor how little in accord with even the Israeli bourgeoisie. Cheap labour, he was saying, and the cost-of-living index tied to wages, left it wide open to manufac-turers, especially with all the new immigrants coming in hungry for jobs and possessions, and what with govern-ment subsidies up to 80 per cent for new enterprises, no union troubles with Histadrut because it was the same as the government more or less, what more could you ask for? By comparison, America was saturated, the old-timers had got a stranglehold on it, holding the ring closed for the

profiteering businessmen and politicians. To come to Israel
had been the best decision of his life: more rumpling of
Sima's hair, just as she was getting up to fetch the bowl of
fruit salad. We were in the middle of eating this when
Sima's father, the famous tycoon, arrived, a ratty, bony man
who looked with unconcealed disapproval at the idle figures
lying round the pool with their plates emptying before
them. Refusing the fruit salad, he took a cup of coffee. By
the time that he had drunk it down Norbert had reappeared,
having changed into a tropical beige suit, and he came back
on to the lawn with a briefcase under his arm. His father-in-
law hardly bothered to nod his head at the guests, but
pecked at Sima's cheek as he left. So did Norbert, stooping
as if in imitation. A black Mercedes swept them out of the
short drive and away down the coast towards the industrial
city. When they had gone, Sima turned to us with a small
smile, excusing Norbert for having to work so hard. Then
I dared go into the house to switch off the hi-fi and in the
surprising peace, we continued to lie around the swimming
pool under the steady sun.

Chapter Ten

THE LAST WORD

ONCE, SHORTLY AFTER MY arrival in Israel, I said to a
friend that I had been in Germany as a soldier, and I saw
her stiffen, saw her eyes widen. Several months later, when
I got to know her better, she told me that she had indeed
recoiled at this unexpected contact, at the ambiguous
possibility which I might represent. I had nearly touched on
things which are not spoken about so directly, or if they are
discussed, then the first person is excluded. Survivors from
the holocaust, from the camps, are known to talk about
their experiences to one another, and those who have ever
listened to such a dialogue say that although there is so
much inevitable involvement yet the tone is mostly one of
reminiscence; a hideous parody, it seems, of an old boys'
reunion. Of course the disaster is frequently mentioned, but
usually in its more abstract connotations. Many times I sat
up late into the nights arguing about patterns in history,
anti-Semitism, genocide, weighing the supposed barbarism
of the Germans as a racial characteristic against more
temporal factors of politics and nationalism and unemploy-
ment. In such a broad framework of ideas the mind can
intellectualize and rationalize, and it takes the easy way out
gratefully. Personal suffering is too painful and dignified for
autobiography, defying the fact of extermination. In Hannah
Arendt's book about the Eichmann trial, one sentence near
the beginning stood out: 'As witness followed witness and
horror was piled on horror, they sat there and listened in

public to stories they would hardly have been able to endure in private, when they would have had to face the story-teller.' Hence the intellectual debates and passions, the thesis and the antithesis, the attempts at mastering the chaos to which one always comes back in the end. Hence, too, the official language, rhetorical and portentous, and even the propaganda on such a subject, and the newspaper bombast and the atrocity books with gaudy covers unsold on the stalls. To generalize is to avoid particularizing; it is to cover each single unthinkable murder with an acceptable form. It works effectively too until one takes in a passer-by along the street, noticing at the same glance his trousers stretched by a paunch, his rolled sleeves and the blue tattooed numbers on his forearm; or until one hears German spoken, or makes a remark about one's national service. Then one wonders how there can be so much normality and acceptance, or rather, can anybody ever be normal again after such an experience? And anyone in a contiguous relation to this experience asks this question too. The most vivid, because the most unexpected, illustration came one sunny afternoon when I realized that the neighbours in a house which I had been lent were also people to whom I had a letter of introduction, and so I called round. As we walked in their large garden, and I was shown their collection of Palestine antiquities, the conversation eased, as if naturally, from my impressions of Israel to anti-Semitism. They were Israelis of several generations' standing, but in the pretty garden with a table set for tea and ice-cream, and Roman statuary around, all the evidence of their security, this was what they wished to talk about to a stranger.

From there it is a short step to feeling that all this bustle and business, productivity and success, is a routine compensation device for a morbid melancholy, a vast permeating sadness and neurosis. So one looks again at this sunburnt young man running to catch a bus with his briefcase bulging open, at that sexy, well-built girl sucking at a straw in a lemonade bottle and staring back, at the column of naughty

shouting children in identical blue uniforms being shep-
herded across the street, at the couples volleying rubber
balls on the crowded beaches. If it is all compensation, then
somehow it has managed to topple over into energy, into
life.

When I arrived in Israel, Eichmann's protracted trial was
over and he had already been sentenced to death, a judgement against which he had appealed. Although his guilt and
the subsequent sentence were the natural presuppositions
to the kidnapping, few people seemed to accept his execution
as something inevitable and logical. Under the appeals for
mercy, and the arguments that it could be no retribution to
kill just one more man however responsible, that the
Israelis should set an example, that their history justified
some great action of pardon, and more refined still, that the
execution of Eichmann might resolve the collective German
guilt, all certainty began to shred away. Also the tension of
the trial had wound down after the court had risen, as if to
provide an interlude before the last drama. As was only to
be expected during the trial, the survivors and their families
had followed every turn, listening to the evidence which was
broadcast on the wireless, thereby making public the things
which are not discussed. The circumstances, the renewed
collision of facts and emotions, the reunion, appeared to
have brought to the surface a latent hysteria. I heard of an
occasion in Haifa when the thirty passengers of a bus had
spontaneously burst into tears as they listened to the testi-
mony of one witness which was being relayed just then.
Buses had apparently been specially provided with wire-
lesses. People hurried home from work in order not to miss
a word; they collected all the newspaper reports.

Perhaps this was another difference of generations. Older
people participated in this trial, lived it. It liberated them
from their repressions, their memories, by enlarging the
immediate range of those with first-hand experience, or
something like it, by bringing these horrors officially into
the open and observing judges, ministers and authorities

in general trying to shoulder the burden, wrestling some real meaning into the abstract language. To look at the past through their eyes was in the nature of a catharsis. If, then, this was meant to be a show trial in the sense that Gentiles and Arabs would draw the conclusions that anti-Semitism would never again go unpunished, it was not a success, for the internal effect came to overshadow any other consideration. Nobody bothered to think what might be the result abroad when they were preoccupied in their own past. No doubt the trial was also intended for the younger generation which is supposed to be largely unaware of its own formative inheritance, and no doubt, too, it was beyond them; it belonged to another continent, to another way of life: it was the affair of their parents. Vengeance, justice, these were the resulting emotions they could understand, helping to bridge the gulf of experience, wiping out the history which stares down so brutally and incomprehensibly from the museum and memorial walls, and merging it into the future which their parents shaped for them in direct contrast. 'But where was our army?' is the poignant, inescapable question which a fifteen-year-old Israeli asks, and the truthful answer seems to separate present and past more irrevocably than anything else.

This was memorably shown to me one day in Jerusalem, in the central hall of the Yad Vashem memorial to those who were killed in the death camps, when I saw two women in tears before some of the documents on permanent exhibition while immediately behind them a group of school-children, who were being taken round, had to be kept in order and made to pay attention by their teacher and an official guide who had come over to them scandalized at their noise. But in the university where I was staying at the time something not far removed in reaction could be found. One evening in May I was invited to a party in the Rassco housing development, on the outskirts of the town, where the grey blocks march up a Jerusalem hillside. It was in a student's room, with a fat man strumming at the piano, and the rest of us singing the songs we knew and improvising others. Chairs borrowed from the other flats on the staircase had been crammed into the small room; and soon the sofa collapsed under half a dozen perching guests. I went into the kitchen to find a drink and met three graduates who had taken refuge there. They were talking about a rumour that Buber was intending to give a public lecture demanding clemency for Eichmann (as he and other faculty members did indeed later petition the authorities), and one of them, an American who was now a religious student at a *yeshiva*, was holding that it was irrelevant to contemporary Israel to bring Eichmann to trial; to be answered that the affair would do Israel nothing but harm in the rest of the world, and that Eichmann therefore ought to be deported to Germany where nobody need bother about him again, since that was the way they felt. Back in the other room, the fat man was accompanying himself to sugary waltzes and pop-songs, he might even have been making them up for he slipped in passages in the grand manner, skilfully covering up for the broken notes of the piano. After a while couples began to dance; the room was too small for more than two or three at a time, so the rest of us watched them. The Eichmann conversation interested none of them.

At the end of May, when Eichmann was due to appear before the Court of Appeal to hear the final verdict, I was living in Tel Aviv. As the time drew near, the tension began to mount; the newspapers took a renewed interest, the foreign journalists returned. On an excursion one day someone took me out of the way in order to drive past the prison at Ramleh where Eichmann was held. It was a motley yellow British-style fortress with a surround of barbed wire and the usual guard-posts and watch-towers. But there was a knot of sightseers, those people who crowd round at anything, not for a positive reason, to think or to observe, but just to stand and by waiting to bring on the next moment, whatever it is. In Tel Aviv one went over the well-worn arguments once again: all the nuances, the shifts of emphasis that in their turn were generalizations, academic heavings designed to obscure the central fact that a criminal was brought to justice, seen to be brought to justice, and there was only one possible outcome. But speculation is the conscience's tranquillizer, soothing together the problem and the worry, so that I do not think I would have made an effort to get to the court unless I had been informed that a seat would possibly be available on application.

The drive from Tel Aviv to Jerusalem is a kind of metaphor for the whole country, a bouncy strip edging along the Jordan border until it swings inland through the Jerusalem corridor, passing down a valley in which the burnt-out hulks of lorries and armoured cars have been placed by the roadside as a memorial to the 1948 siege and the ambushed relief convoys. I had not taken the precaution beforehand of finding out where the trial was being held and so I drove into the centre of Jerusalem through a crowded market towards the main street. Life was as usual, there were no signposts to the court and nothing in the pace or activity of the streets to indicate that anything was happening. When I asked the way, nobody seemed to have any idea what I could be referring to, until someone finally explained that the trial was held in the new Beth Ha'am, the House of the People. By the time I arrived, I was almost late. The street outside this modern building was virtually empty, there were few parked cars. I hurried past two elderly women dressed in black and heard one of them say, 'It's our last day'. The entrance was protected by wire netting and was guarded by police. Showing my entry card, I was allowed to cross the small courtyard into a row of wooden booths where I was frisked, and then I followed the other late-comers up flights of stairs, running to take my place high up at the back of the courtroom. It was a large featureless place, aseptic and dull, built rather like a modern cinema, with tiers rising back almost to the roof. On a mounted stage where the screen might have been, were the judges and

below them to their right was the notorious glass cage in
which Eichmann sat. He was therefore visible to the public
only in profile and he took care not to turn in their direction.
But he was afflicted with a severe nervous tic, so violent that
he must have been suffering from it for a good many years,
and sometimes he seemed to shake himself towards us. Even
at this distance, though, it was clear that he did not look
like the next man, as the journalists had mostly reported,
but that he was sallow, saturnine and mean-featured. A long
thin mouth cut under a long thin nose. But the judge was
already beginning to read aloud. I saw that a good many
in the audience were listening to him over earphones which
provided simultaneous translation from the Hebrew into
German, French and English, and I returned as fast as
possible down the flights of stairs to fetch a pair from a desk
near the entrance, to run breathless back again to my seat,
and certain that the opening words which I had missed
would turn out to be essential. The judge had a thick document in front of him, which proved to be an amplification
of the earlier judgement of the District Court and one which
set the burden of responsibility for the genocide even more
firmly on Eichmann. Most of its substance, however, was
legal precedence and argument and its language was not
easy for the layman to follow. As the long sentences
succeeded one another, the discrepancy between the crimes
and the available remedies grew almost fantastic: the
generalizations had taken control, until even the emotions
of justice could only be thought of polysyllabically. All too
soon I was beginning to compare the translations, switching
from one language to another. The German, to which
Eichmann was presumably listening, sounded to me incom-
parably the clumsiest and the most hesitant. Stepping over
the legal points which I had missed and concentrating, I
determined to follow more accurately the problem of one
country's rights within the territory of another. All the
instances, kidnapping, piracy, sounded so improbable out
of their context. The courtroom was becoming oppressively

hot and drowsy. Next to me was a small man with a bony sunburnt face, hard and glistening as if carved from wood. He sat immobile with his hat on his lap, and quite soon he had imperceptibly nodded off to sleep. His wife, a fat woman who spread out of her chair, would dig him with her elbow. Nor was he the only person to succumb to the stuffiness. In front of us was a row of men and women, all the same bulbous shape, keeping up a muttered conversation among themselves, but now and again one of them would slip forward in his seat as he dozed off. The audience on this occasion was remarkably uniform. They were nearly all middle-aged or elderly people and the very few young men I saw were mostly orthodox Jews. If there were any *kibbutzniks*, they had dressed up for the trial in suit and tie, but my impression was that the country at large had decided not to attend, not to send representatives. It was a local occasion. Perhaps it was because they were mostly elderly that they were overcome by the poor ventilation, but by the time that the judge had read half his document, many people needed to be shaken by the shoulder by the policemen circulating in the courtroom.

The legal voice read on and the man in the glass cage twitched from time to time. He had the intensity of a carrion bird. He would moisten his lips, and once or twice he took down a note. The even tone had settled over the courtroom, unfolding the improbable episodes of Turkish ships in collision, *Regina* v. . . . , (1873), Geneva and Mr Justice So-and-so's decision. Suddenly the verdict; the courtroom stiffened for five minutes until it was all over; the wooden face of the man beside me never altered; the cage was empty; the policemen were clearing us all out, and with the surprised hum of released talk, we all trooped downstairs, to stand blinking in the midday sun outside. A light breeze relieved the heat, but brought with it strong petrol fumes from the town. Journalists seethed into the press room; a queue waited to hand back the earphones, I noticed the two elderly women dressed in black, still standing where they had been as I entered. Groups of people came together and drifted apart, dispersing as if they were looking for a purpose. Taking a transcription of the proceedings, I walked away into the centre of the town, to look for iced coffee. One expected the event of this trial to be marked in some way, but later when I returned to my car, the streets were empty, there was not even a policeman, and only the little wooden booths were a reminder of what had happened. Everything else had swirled away into the life of Jerusalem.

The appeal for mercy was rejected by the President and within forty-eight hours Eichmann was hanged. There was no time for deliberation, for more generalization. This was the long-awaited action. After his death I do not remember talking about the trial again: there was nothing further to discuss.

GLOSSARY

Agudat Yisrael. Association of Israel; the political party of the ultra-orthodox religious community in Israel.

Aliyah (*lit.* "going up"). Jewish immigration to Israel.

Ashkenazi (*pl.* Ashkenazim). A descendant of Jews who once lived in Germany; applied generally to Jews from Northern, Central and Eastern Europe.—Ashkenazic, *adj.*

Balfour Declaration. A declaration issued by the British foreign secretary, Lord Balfour, in November, 1917, declaring that the British government views favorably the eventual establishment of a Jewish national home in Palestine.

Bnei Brith, or B'nai B'rith (*lit.* "sons of covenant"). An American Jewish fraternal and service organization.

Druze. A member of a non-Arabic people living principally in Lebanon and Syria, but also in Israel.

dunam. A land measure equal to approximately one-quarter acre.

Egged. One of the principal Israeli bus companies.

the Emek (*lit.* "valley"). The Valley of Jezreel.

Eretz Israel (*lit.* "Land of Israel"). Palestine.

Essenes. An ancient Jewish monastic sect.

fedayeen (*pl.*). Members of an anti-Israel Arab commando group that often carries out raids in Israeli territory.

Gadna. An Israeli youth organization whose members often spend vacation or holiday time in volunteer agricultural work, predraft military training, etc.

gifilte fish (*lit.* "stuffed fish"). A fish dish popular among Jews from Central and Eastern Europe.

Goyim (*pl.*). Gentiles.

Habimah. A major Israeli theatrical company.

Hagana (*lit.* "defence"). The Israeli army. *In full* Israel Defence Army.

Hassidism. The practice of an orthodox mystical sect of Judaism founded in eighteenth-century Poland.—Hassidic, *adj.*

Histadrut (*lit.* "federation"). General Federation of Labour; the organization of Israeli trade unions.

horah. A folk dance considered the Israeli national dance.

Irgun (*lit.* "organization"). National Military Organization; in British Palestine, an underground Jewish military and terroristic group.

Keren Kayemet. A land development agency in Israel. *Also called* Jewish National Fund.

kibbutz (*pl.* kibbutzim). A collective settlement, generally agricultural, where a high degree of communal living is practised.

kibbutznik. A member of a kibbutz.

Knesset. The parliament of the state of Israel.

lebanya. A cultured milk product; yoghurt.

maarbaroth (*pl.*). Temporary villages for new immigrants.

Mapai. Israel Workers' Party; Israel's largest political party.

Mapam. United Workers' Party; a left-wing Zionist political party.

matzos (*pl.*). Unleavened bread eaten by Jews on the Passover.

Mea Shearim. The orthodox quarter in Jerusalem.

Mizrachi. National Religious Party; a political party of orthodox Jews.

mukhtar. The head of an Arab village.

Nahal. A division of the Israeli army whose members serve part of their period of military training living and working on a border kibbutz.

moshav. A co-operative agricultural settlement or village.

Neturei Karta (*lit.* "guardians of the city"). An organization of ultra-orthodox Jews.

Pale. In Tsarist Russia, the area of western Russia and Poland to which Jewish settlement was restricted.

Palmach. In British Palestine and the early years of the state of Israel, a commando division of the Jewish military forces.

Pesach. The Festival of Passover; a feast commemorating the biblical exodus from Egypt.

Purim. The Feast of Lots; a holiday commemorating the success of Esther and Mordecai in the biblical book of Esther.

Rab. A traditional Hebrew title of respect.

rehov. Street.

sabra (*lit.* "prickly pear"). A native-born Israeli.

Sephardi (*pl.* Sephardim). A descendant of Jews who once lived in Spain; applied generally to Jews from North Africa and the Levant. —Sephardic, *adj.*

shikunim (*pl.*). Housing developments.

shtetl. A little town in the Russian or Polish Pale of Jewish settlement.

souk. An Arab market-place.

tarbush. A cap commonly worn by Moslem men.

ulpan. A school for new immigrants for the intensive study of the Hebrew language; often part of an agricultural settlement so that time is divided between study and work.

vatikim (*pl.*). The older members of a community.

wadi. A valley or ravine; also a river bed usually dry except for the rainy season.

Yad Vashem. An Institution in Jerusalem for the preservation of data, cultural materials, etc. concerning European Jewry destroyed during World War II.

yeshiva. A school, or academy, of orthodox religious instruction.

Yiddish. A Germanic language mainly spoken by Jews from Eastern Europe.

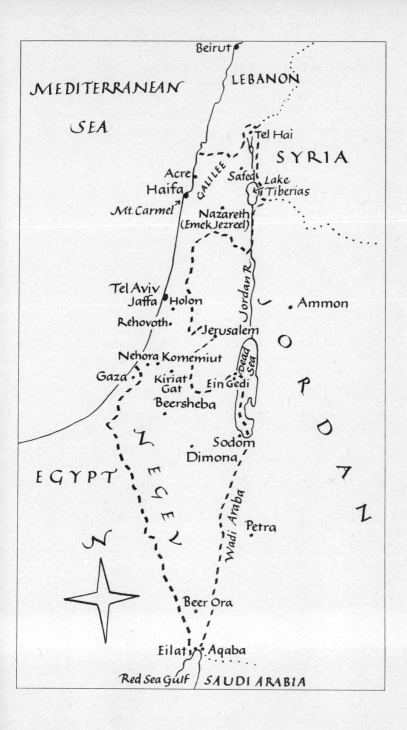